CARS CARS
CARS CARS

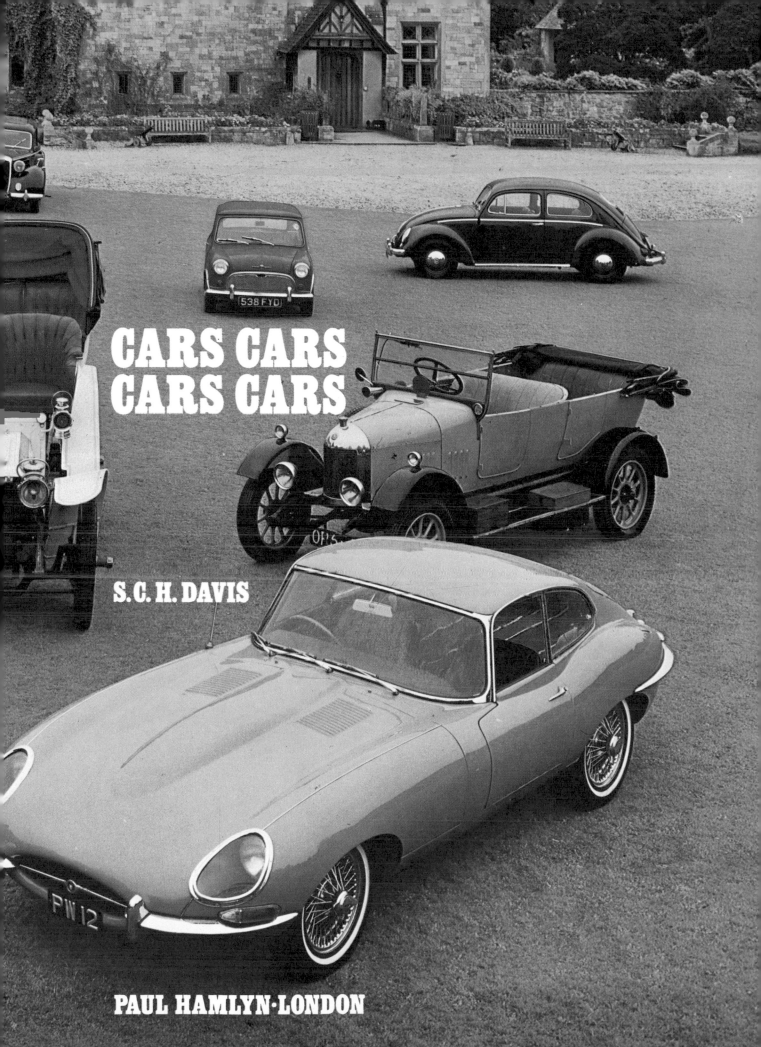

CARS CARS CARS CARS

S. C. H. DAVIS

PAUL HAMLYN·LONDON

Published by
THE HAMLYN PUBLISHING GROUP LTD
Hamlyn House – The Centre –
Feltham – Middlesex
© 1967 The Hamlyn Publishing Group Ltd
First edition 1967
Second impression 1968
Printed in Italy by Arnoldo Mondadori Editore - Verona

CONTENTS

BEGINNINGS

Left: A Panhard of 1893, a four-seater 'omnibus'. This must be one of the very first attempts at closed coachwork. It has glass windows all round, except for the front sides, where the driver and passengers would enter.

The beginnings of the motor car are shrouded in mystery, since exact data is extremely hard to come by, and legend arising after the event is inevitable. Moreover, scores of men throughout the world each contributed a little knowledge from which further development logically created the machines we know today.

Engines, as engines, began with curious experiments, details of which are naturally lost in the mists of antiquity for no one thought them important at the time. Two centuries before Christ, Hero of Alexandria, for example, is said to have made a sphere turn on an axle by using jets of steam – but it came to nothing. In 1678 Father Verbiest, a missionary in China, thought out a little steam-driven 'chariot' to amuse his protector, Nan-Ho-Ay-Gin. Five years earlier, Christian Huygens had made steam operate a piston in a cylinder. But these are only three of countless men who, throughout the centuries, made innumerable experiments – many of them totally useless, many adding only a little to the slow process of evolution of the modern machine, but the few making great and significant discoveries.

Nowadays news of any of these exciting experiments would be circulated all over the world by the daily papers. But way back in the early days of engines news circulated only by chance meeetings between people, or perhaps by a letter if the subject was thought interesting enough to set down on paper. Consequently, engine development took place in Europe and America, even in France and Britain, individually, and independently, and no one engineer knew what was happening in any other country.

In Britain James Watt, who was trained in the making of precision instruments, and greatly encouraged by Glasgow University, began to think about steam engines. We are all taught the legend that Watt's idea for using steam originated from watching the lid of his grandmother's kettle moving up and down under steam pressure. Whether this is true or not, Watt, who was in poor health as a boy and so religious that he would not continue even the most interesting experiment on a Sunday, was asked to repair a model of a very crude engine designed by Thomas Newcomen around 1705. Briefly this engine operated by admitting steam at low pressure into a cylinder below a very light piston. Steam then drove the piston up. When the piston reached the top of the cylinder a jet of water was squirted into the steam to condense it and form a vacuum. As the top of the cylinder was open, atmospheric pressure drove the piston down again. Watt decided to use steam pressure only to drive the engine

One of the first Benz cars of 1886. The machine has three wheels, thus simplifying the steering gear. The single-cylinder engine was intended to run at a steady speed, hence the huge, horizontal flywheel. The water was cooled in the vertical tank shown—there is no radiator—and the drive was by belts and chains.

The Dudgeon Steam Wagon. It was built by Richard Dudgeon of New York in 1886, was used for the next six years, and in 1903 it ran in a trial at 10 m.p.h. Called the 'Red Devil', its drive was by steam without benefit of gearing. The wheels are of solid cedar with iron tyres. The engineer is provided with a seat apart to tend the fire.

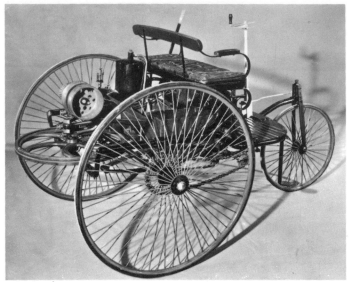

and the advantage was immediately apparent. But he was unable to continue his experiments owing to financial trouble. In 1768 he first met Matthew Boulton, who was not only very intelligent but rich, with whom a year later he formed the Birmingham firm of Boulton and Watt. However, this company produced only practical, stationary steam engines, but progress towards a road vehicle at last became realistic.

It became a reality when Joseph Cugnot developed a steam vehicle. Born in Lorraine in 1725, Cugnot worked at the French Military School at Mezières. It happened that his immediate superior, de Gribeauval, was in the service of the Duke de Choiseul. These two encouraged and financed Cugnot in his endeavour to make a steam tractor for towing artillery. Progress was beset by obstacles, both political and financial, but Cugnot persisted. About that time, the revolution in France had disposed of the monarchy and the whole country was in chaos. But by 1800 Cugnot's strange steam-driven, three-wheeled tractor was in the main French arsenal under the control of Roland. Roland had become Commissaire Général of the artillery under Napoleon and had used all his influence to forward the advantages of the tractor. So, on 24th January, 1800, the tractor was tested officially. It ran well, though briefly, in Vincennes Park; or at least so it was reported at the time. Napoleon, in point of fact, was far too busy leading France's armies to take a real interest in this new mechanical carriage, and thus missed being connected with the birth of mechanically propelled road vehicles.

In America progress continued without European liaison and proceeded so well that in 1805 a strange

contraption was actually seen running slowly along a road in Philadelphia, a vehicle with a steam engine driving not only the wheels but a paddle astern, for its crude body was watertight enough for it to swim as well as run on the road. All of this was due to Oliver Evans, but his unhappy reward was to be considered not quite right in the head.

Back again in Britain steam had made further advances. One of Watt's men, Murdock, made a model, steam-driven three-wheeler in 1786 which could actually run, though it achieved no further progress. But in 1827 a monstrous affair, made as much like a four horse coach as possible, was actually driven down the road from London to Bath at an average of six m.p.h. This formidable vehicle was designed by a Cornishman, Goldsworthy Gurney, who by profession was a surgeon but who had become violently enthusiastic about mechanical transport on the road. Behind the coach body was the boiler and engine; most of the passengers sat on the roof while the unfortunate driver was seated right in front, and attempted to steer with a long handle. In 1833 cumbersome steam coaches designed by Walter Hancock were being run as a passenger service on the roads between Oxford Street, London and Edgware, Regents Circus and Uxbridge.

But the state of Britain's roads, the absence of pneumatic tyres, and the violent opposition from almost everyone in the country to the idea of mechanical propulsion ensured failure for all these early efforts.

The true beginning of the car as we know it today was in the year 1885, in Germany. Karl Benz, a watch mechanic and the son of a steam engineer, had a friend named Walter, who was a printer. Walter had trouble

But the car which became most famous in the early days was this four-wheeled Benz of 1900. Deemed reliable for its day, this model has a single-cylinder, three h.p. engine, tiller-steering and reasonably good brakes. The small lever projecting from the steering-column operated a very low, emergency, planetary gear.

with his feet, and tried to ride one of the earliest bicycles but with catastrophic results. So he gave the solid-tyred machine to Benz, who immediately decided that it should have an engine and, for safety, another wheel. The result was the first of a few experimental cars in 1885 and 1886, followed in 1891 by a full four-wheeler. All these machines ran well, if slowly.

Benz's knowledge of engines stemmed from experience with the oil or gas engines of that time, which ran at about 130 revolutions a minute. Reciprocating engines were being used a good deal at that time for pumping, driving line-shafting for workshops and other various jobs, most of them having large single-cylinder engines run on paraffin oil or coal gas. For the Benz engine a mixture of air and petrol was formed in a tank, called a carburetter, and sucked through a valve into a cylinder when the piston in the latter was going down. Immediately the piston began to return on the up-stroke, the inlet valve closed and the gas was compressed. At full compression an electric spark fired the gas which drove the piston down. When the piston returned once more another valve was opened, so the burned gas escaped to the open air. As soon as the gas had had time to escape the exhaust valve closed, the inlet valve opened, and the engine received a fresh charge of gas.

This cycle of operations was quite different from that of the steam engine. For the latter, steam under pressure

René Panhard with his wife and children in a Panhard
'Dog-cart' of 1892. The firm of Panhard & Levassor acquired
the rights to sell Daimler engines in France, and in
this way entered the car-manufacturing field. If one
compares this 'Dog-cart' with the model on page 10 it can
be seen just how rapidly these cars were developing.

Top: This Peugeot of 1892 was obviously influenced by Benz design, but was a definite step forward as regards comfort and protection for its occupants. The tiller for steering resembles the handle of a bicycle.
Centre: Henry Ford's first car of 1896. This brakeless, reverseless, two-cylinder buckboard wasn't much of a machine compared with the fairly sophisticated cars in Europe, but it was good enough to get him further finance.
Bottom: By 1888 the Benz had improved considerably, though it still had three wheels. Since the speed of the machine never exceeded 20 m.p.h. and there was little other traffic, the brake in the form of a block was sufficient.

was admitted through one valve to the cylinder and drove the piston down, another valve opened to let the steam out when the piston returned. Sometimes steam was admitted first one side of the piston then the other, thus obtaining more power without increased weight. The steam engine developed power with every revolution of the crankshaft, the petrol engine only did so once in two revolutions of the crankshaft. For the petrol engine the compressed gas could be exploded either by an electric spark from a plug timed to occur on the compression stroke, or by the compressed gas being forced into a white hot platinum tube. To heat the tube a species of blow lamp using petrol was installed.

Benz favoured electric ignition from the first. Since the engine had to be cooled, jackets were cast round the cylinder and filled with water which circulated to a cooling tank or radiator, placed well above the engine, because hot water rises while cold water sinks. Since the machine originated from the concept of a mechanized bicycle it had big wire wheels, solid rubber tyres, rather sketchy brakes, and a tiller by which to steer.

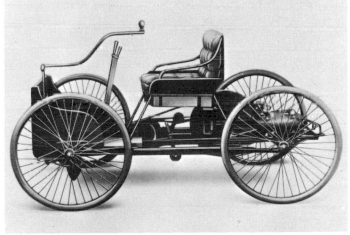

A steam engine develops power without respect to its crankshaft speed, but a petrol engine does not. If the petrol engine has to pull too great a load it slows, and therefore power is reduced. Benz overcame this difficulty by fitting a gear change mechanism, consisting of belts and pulleys which drove the rear axle through a chain, thus providing a low gear to climb hills and a high gear for speed on the flat.

Another German, Gottlieb Daimler, was also busy experimenting with the petrol engine at this time. The second son of a baker, Daimler was a good mechanic with wide experience of the internal combustion engine. His engine differed from that of Benz in having two cylinders rather than one, tube ignition rather than electric, and in a very short time, a 'jet carburetter', i.e. a carburetter with a little jet squirting petrol into a stream of air. It was with this engine that the first Daimler car ran on the road in 1889, and it was obvious at once that it was a carriage in its own right rather than a development of the bicycle.

These cars had very little power, possibly because there was still a tendency to regard mechanical horse power as representing the power of live horses, and therefore three h.p. should suffice. And speed, as speed, was not yet considered, all that was hoped for was the pace usually associated with horse vehicles. But the effect of the Benz and Daimler was immense.

Meantime much was happening in the United States. George B. Selden, having come over to Europe in 1870

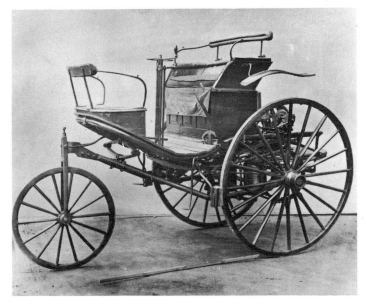

Top: A very gaily decorated Peugeot of 1892. The passengers sit facing each other. This Peugeot model in fact quickly started a short-lived fashion for decorating and painting any make of car with pretty and often fantastic designs.

Centre: The ancestor of all the Fiats. It was built in 1899, and powered by a 3½ h.p. engine. It is seen here taking a leisurely and fashionable drive round the park.
Bottom: A very early type of American New Orleans car of the 1890s.

and seen what was being developed there, turned his attention to the power-driven road vehicle, eventually obtaining a patent for a 'motor car'. Selden seems to have been a man with more enthusiasm than engineering knowledge, but with a strong sense of future financial gain. He claimed that he had designed a car with a petrol engine in 1877. But there seems to be no independent authority or witness for this claim. What we do know is that he asked for a patent in 1879 and that it was not granted until November, 1895, presumably because he was unable to produce evidence that such a car had been built. But, and this was where the trouble arose, the patent covered any vehicle with an engine using petrol. For years afterwards this was a thorn in the side of the infant car industry in America, as well as a hindrance to those who wanted to import a car from Europe. It seemed as though Selden had 'cornered' the car industry in the United States. In 1903 Selden even attacked that genius Henry Ford, claiming royalties, but in the subsequent vitriolic law suit – lasting until 1911 – he met his match, for the case was resolved in Henry Ford's favour. Incidentally Ford claimed in after years that he had made a car which ran in 1891, though all the evidence suggests that it really appeared in 1895!

The real start of the huge American industry was due more certainly to Charles and Frank Duryea. They created a very spidery affair in 1895, having already had vast trouble with an engine built in 1892. It is interesting that one of these Duryea cars, looking rather like Queen Victoria's pony cart without its pony or shafts, did take part in the run from London to Brighton organized in Britain on 14th November, 1896, to celebrate the passing of a new law freeing the car from many previous restrictions. This event was the reason for the subsequent annual London to Brighton Run now organized by the Royal Automobile Club.

But from 1895 onwards progress in Europe was speedy and practical, the day of the wild but untrained enthusiast had gone. A French wood-working firm called Panhard had been persuaded to build cars and were using the Daimler engine. Daimler himself now had the assistance of a very able engineer, Maybach, a partnership which produced the famous V two-cylinder engine called a Daimler-Phenix, that could develop as much as six h.p. and was probably the finest engine of that period. However, the first Panhard of 1890 was a much cruder affair than the cars which made history, though nevertheless a machine of promise, as none could deny.

Right: The Hon. Evelyn Ellis at the tiller of an 1897 British Daimler, which was apparently constructed from the drawings of the German car, in a converted mill-building at Coventry. The rear passengers are facing backwards, an idea which was quite usual in those days, and which was a direct inheritance from the horse-drawn carriage. After this machine the British Daimler developed along its own lines.

Goldsworthy Gurney's Steam Carriage of 1827.
It carried six passengers inside and 12 outside, and the front boot carried the luggage. Just in front of the rear wheels there are 'legs' which Gurney fitted 'to help upon hills'. The carriage was capable of speeds upwards of 15 m.p.h. These early steam coaches failed because of the extremely bad road surfaces, the almost universal antagonism towards them in Britain and the great difficulty of steering such cumbersome machines.

Top: The British engineer Frederick Lanchester was always obstinately original, as this picture of the first Lanchester car of 1895 shows. It was designed to run at 15 m.p.h., and though it was more comfortable than its rivals and steered remarkably well, it did not have sufficient power to climb hills with more than one aboard.

Bottom: An eight h.p. Fiat of 1900-1902. This has a hood for the driver and passenger, but the seat at the back is at the mercy of the elements.

Top: James Watt, the engineer, had an assistant, William Murdock, who made this model for a steam carriage in 1786. It worked well, but Watt was furious that his assistant should waste time in this fashion. So a most promising idea was shelved for ever.
Centre: A Morris and Salom Electric taxi cab, which ran on the New York streets in the 1890s. They were the world's first horseless hansom cabs.
Bottom: The De Dion motor tricycle of 1898 was one of the most consistently reliable machines. Countless motorists started driving with these models.

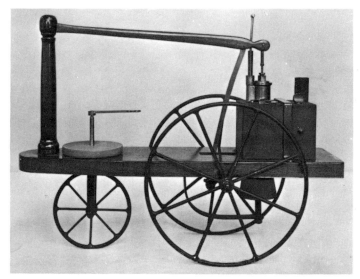

Panhard were followed in 1892 by Peugeot, for whose car also the Daimler engine was used. The original firm of Peugeot grew from a firm called Les Fils de Peugeot Frères de Valentigny, run by the Peugeot family, with factories then engaged in making coffee machines. These factories had then come under the control of Armand Peugeot and his cousin Eugène Peugeot. Initially these two were interested in the new vehicles by the wood-working factory of Périn-Panhard from which the famous firm of Panhard & Levassor was to spring. Furthermore a Daimler motor company had been started in Britain and in 1897 produced their first version of the German car.

The first four-cylinder German Daimler appeared in 1898; it was improved by magneto ignition in 1899 and also provided with pneumatic tyres – a great step forward. Magneto ignition was a small, compact device which consisted of large horseshoe-shaped magnets between which revolved an armature driven from the engine. On the armature were two wire windings one of which developed low tension current similar to that supplied from a battery. When a contact breaker cut off this current suddenly, the result was to create very high tension current in the second winding. This high tension current created a spark between the points of a sparking plug, and the spark ignited the compressed gas in the engine cylinder. If the engine had more than one cylinder a revolving arm, fed with this high tension current, switched the current to one of the plugs concerned. The high tension current distributor and the contact breaker were in one assembly, driven by gears from the armature shaft. This in fact was not only simpler than the hot tube ignition previously used by Daimler but more reliable than the battery-fed ignition of the Benz.

Meantime Benz had developed the famous 3½ h.p., four-wheeler, two-seater, which first appeared in 1894. Fragile though this car might be, with its wire wheels and solid tyres, it nevertheless ran remarkably well and was the first attempt to make a machine at low cost (2,000 Marks, about £200) for general use. The engine was in the rear compartment, had one cylinder of nearly two litres' capacity, battery ignition with a 'trembler coil', a very crude system for cooling and a surface carburetter.

A 'trembler coil' was an amusing idea. The coil was, as usual, a box containing two coils of wire so arranged that if current passing through one was interrupted suddenly, very high voltage current was created in the other and sent to the sparking plug. In the centre of

Louis Renault, famous pioneer from the heroic age of motoring. It was due to the Renault family's concentration on designing a smaller engine that attracted particular attention, especially when Marcel, Louis' brother, won the Paris-Vienna race of 1902 against much larger-engined cars.

Karl Benz, the German engineer, who first succeeded in making the 'horseless carriage' a practical proposition. His early designs were much influenced by attempts to fit a motor to a friend's tricycle. Hence his first car of 1885 was still a tricycle with slender wire wheels.

the coils of wire was a long magnet. When current from the battery was passed to the coil by a contact breaker the magnet attracted a blade spring. On the blade spring was a contact through which the current passed on the way to the coil. When the magnet attracted the blade the current was switched off. Instantly the blade spring returned to its original position thereby switching the current on again, a process rapidly repeated so long as the contact breaker permitted. This produced a stream of sparks at the plug instead of a single spark. In error it was thought that this made the firing of the compressed gas in the cylinder more reliable, whereas experience has taught us this is a fallacy.

Still the gear ratio change was made by shifting a belt from one set of pulleys to another, the belt-driven shaft driving the rear wheels by chains. There was also an emergency low gear called a 'Crypto', which the driver could use by pulling up a handle. This gear did not need any skill to handle, though the result of too much verve with the control handle has been known to

jerk the Benz vigorously forward on its rear wheels only, its front wheels up high in the air. There was a feeble pedal-operated brake, but the driver relied upon the very good hand brake. Curiously enough this was one of the first cars in which the driver sat on the right, most others having the driver on the left.

One more pioneer was to have a great effect on motoring generally: a Frenchman, the Count de Dion. He had already spent considerable time and money experimenting with steam-driven tricycles and steam generally, and he turned to the petrol engine in 1885. The Count was eventually to become famous when the firm of De Dion-Bouton started manufacturing small two-seater cars, at a time when most firms were engaged in large car manufacture.

But France and Germany were not to have it all their own way. In Italy a company was formed which was to grow to a huge size, and be responsible for an enormous number of cars of all types, while making for itself a name famous throughout motoring history.

Drawings of Trevithick's Steam Carriage. This curious vehicle was designed by Richard Trevithick in 1802, and actually ran on the road near London for 10 miles. At that time much interest was centred on steam locomotives, running on rails, so his vehicle caused quite a sensation.

Gottlieb Daimler, a pioneer to whom we owe the birth of the first practical engine, which set the type to be used in cars of the future. Not only was Daimler responsible for the German Daimler cars, but with Maybach he designed those magnificent machines to be known as Mercedes some years later.

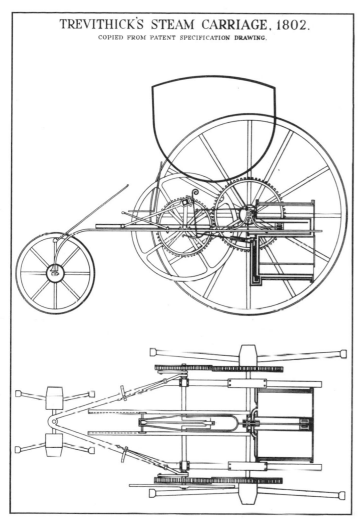

TREVITHICK'S STEAM CARRIAGE, 1802.
COPIED FROM PATENT SPECIFICATION DRAWING.

This was the Fabbrica Italiana Automobili Torino, known today as Fiat. In July, 1899 a group of Turin notables met and founded the Fiat firm. In the works at the edge of Valentino Park, Turin, fifty workmen produced the first Fiat, a two-cylinder small car on conventional lines which was the ancestor of monster Fiats and tiny Fiats alike.

It may be thought strange that no one had yet even considered designing a car with a saloon-type body, or any other form of real protection for the future owner and his family. Panhard had made a car with a closed body in 1895, Daimler one earlier still. But for all that almost all cars had open bodies.

But it is all too easy to judge the ideas of the past with the knowledge of today. Firstly the people who had money to buy those early cars in Europe were for the most part 'gentlemen'. Men of this class had made the control of the horse-drawn vehicle an art full of little things which could be 'done' or 'not done'. A man was judged by the way he handled the ribbons

(reins), and by his strict adherence to essential etiquette. The one thing such people would not do was to drive a closed vehicle; a Berlin, a Brougham, a Landau, or the like. Such carriages were driven by professional coachmen dressed in livery with heraldic badges. The 'Master' could then recline in studied elegance within the vehicle. Only open carriages of the sporting type could be driven personally. Even in the United States much of this etiquette remained.

Thus there was no demand for a closed body car in those early days. But there was another factor. The engines of that day were not powerful enough to pull a large body offering considerable resistance to a high wind, or, when the route lay over steep gradients, any body heavier than an open four-seater. True, the cars had gears which could be changed from those giving a high ratio to those with a lower ratio, but this was by no means an easy job, since, except for machines which had belt drive – and they were in the minority – considerable skill was necessary. In order to change gear the

Top: The German Cannstadt Daimler of 1895 had progressed from the spidery cycle-type machine to a carriage. This vehicle has probably had the tiller replaced by a steering-wheel a year or so after it was built.
Centre: By 1898 the Coventry Daimler showed signs of individuality, and had departed considerably from the

German Daimler design. Notably the body is more comfortable and the upholstery of better quality. There are drip-feed lubricators on the dashboard, which fed the main bearings.
Bottom: A Winton racing car of 1903. This model driven by H. Nelson Jackson, took only 63 days to cross the American continent, and was one of the first cars to do so.

driver had to disengage the clutch, free the gear control lever from its retaining notch on a long quadrant by moving a trigger, then move the lever until he could feel the gears touching and wait until he knew they could be engaged quietly. Or alternatively, he would move the lever while judging engine speed entirely by ear and so obtain the same result. The clutch was then let in again, and the engine acceleration was controlled by careful and difficult adjustment of the ignition and carburetter air supply.

The earliest engines had no throttle but a governor which controlled their speed by keeping the exhaust valve off its seat, but this could be put out of action by a lever or pedal called an accelerator, when it was necessary to change to a lower gear. (Incidentally, the throttle of the modern car is often termed an accelera-

tor though there is no longer an engine governor.)
As you may judge, changing to a higher gear was much
easier than changing down to a lower gear. Furthermore
in a heavier body or in a body with greater wind
resistance, gear-changing had to be very accurate and
performed more frequently.

Yet another factor to contend with, was that the
engineers responsible for the design naturally thought
the mechanism too complicated for the car to be
entrusted to men who had no training in its use and no
aptitude for it, and therefore the body of the car was
definitely of secondary importance. And no one, re-
peat no one, even considered that the car might become a vehicle for everyone. Anyway, the engineers
were having quite enough trouble trying to make the
cars reliable, because everything was still experimental

and they were breaking new ground all the time.
It was difficult enough to drive the cars let alone attend
to their mechanical needs. Apart from the gear change,
steering by tiller could be tricky, especially if the road
surface was full of potholes likely to jerk the tiller
out of the driver's hand, or when the deep ruts often
encountered could grip the narrow solid tyres as
though they were in a tramline. To turn right the
driver had to move the tiller hard over to the left,
which, as most tillers were in the centre, meant considerable inconvenience to the passenger on that side.
It was quite usual in these circumstances for the driver
to hand the tiller to the passenger who held it out far
left if the corner was very sharp. I once drove an
Oldsmobile with tiller steering and used this technique
on a sharp right-hand corner. But the passenger did not

Below: The Peugeot Bébé of 1903, a little car which caused much amusement when it was first produced, but which nevertheless suited many people. It was most reliable, if a shade noisy, and quickly became popular in France and Britain. It was in fact a car in miniature, with the normal features of larger machines.

Right: The Brushmobile—a car with an American-sounding name—had a petrol engine, and was built in England around 1904. The British engineer, Critchley, went to this company from Daimlers to develop this car, but only limited numbers were built.

Bottom right: A Columbia Electric car of 1901. Hundreds of Columbia electric taxis had appeared in New York in 1900, but they were not too successful as they were so heavy— the batteries weighed nearly a ton. This is an attractive little car however, and it was possible to travel quite cheaply if one carried a kit to charge the batteries from the overhead wires of the trolley-car lines.

give the tiller back in time, and we plunged headfirst into a very wet ditch.

Although France took to the new cars with enthusiasm, other countries, even the U.S.A. and Germany were suspicious of them. For example, rumours that these machines were highly dangerous spread all through Europe in the early days. This was mainly the fault of the engineers themselves who, when asked, 'How do these things work?' replied, 'The cylinder sucks in a mixture of air and petrol, compresses it, then explodes it'. The word 'explodes' was sufficient to create sales resistance straightaway.

Antagonism was also created by the fact that horses were badly scared when they met one of the new vehicles billowing clouds of dust far and wide. The British, furthermore, did not take to mechanically propelled vehicles at all easily in any case. Way back in 1865 Parliament had passed a law which made it necessary for 'road locomotives' to be accompanied by three persons of whom one preceded the machine carrying a red flag, walking well ahead of the vehicle. This law also limited speed to four m.p.h. in the open country, two m.p.h. in villages or towns, and it gave local authorities power to ban them altogether. Not until 1878 was the severity of this law modified and then each 'locomotive' had to be preceded by a man,

no mention being made of the red flag, and still local authorities were allowed restrictions of their own.

All this might have been aimed at the steam-engined farm machine on large steel-rimmed wheels, but opponents of the motor car claimed vigorously that the same law applied to the new vehicles. How anyone managed to convince Parliament that the law must be altered is impossible to understand. But in 1896 a new law was passed in which cars termed 'light locomotives', were limited to 14 m.p.h., and had to carry a lamp and bell, 'or other instrument,' to give warning of approach. Yet again, however, the local authority was given power to make further restrictions.

Neither in France nor in Europe generally were the restrictions as severe, so it is easy to see why the British motor industry was handicapped from the start. In addition, too many people saw in the new motor cars the chance to get rich quick, with the result that many promising motor concerns of the time suffered from financial crises, and quite often died before they could get under way.

But though motorists in all countries had to take extreme care wherever and however they drove; slowly but very certainly the new vehicles improved and multiplied. The 'stone age' of motoring was already over as the year 1900 dawned.

Top: The chassis of a six-cylinder Napier of 1903.
Centre left: In 1805 Oliver Evans built his famous amphibious, steam-powered dredge, which waddled from the workshop in which he built it, through the streets of Philadelphia and into the river all under its own power.
Centre right: One of the most successful of America's early cars, the Duryea, which first ran in 1895. From the start the Duryeas concentrated on comfort and ease of control.
Bottom: The most famous of all ancient vehicles, Joseph Cugnot's artillery tractor. As the vehicle was intended for transporting guns, no body was fitted. The enormous tank at the front is in fact the steam boiler.

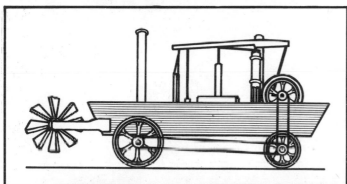

Below: By 1909 the British Vauxhall had changed a lot, and now bore no resemblance to the light, sketchy machine which the original firm of Vauxhall Ironworks first produced. This Vauxhall carries the full equipment of lamps, screen etc., all of which were then extras, but shortly to become standard equipment on all cars..

Bottom: A 1908 Peugeot which had now become one of the best and most famous of French cars. Because there was no universal speed limit in France, and French roads were undeniably more suited to high speeds, French cars developed faster than those in Britain.

Right: Another interesting car, the Prosper-Lambert, a name which has long been forgotten. Despite its name it was actually a French machine, but there were obvious connections with Britain, since the car was quite well known here in 1906.

THE BIRTH OF ELEGANCE

By 1900 the car had become a car, not a variation of the horse-carriage or the cycle, and from this time onwards progress was amazingly rapid. More and more engineers began to show a great deal of interest in the new vehicles, and more and more experiment resulted in invaluable accumulated knowledge.

Much was due to the big races held in France – the Paris-Bordeaux-Paris of 1895 having been followed by the Paris-Marseilles-Paris of 1896, the shorter Paris-Dieppe of 1897, the Paris-Amsterdam-Paris of 1898, the Paris-Bordeaux of 1899, and the Gordon-Bennett in 1900 originated by an American newspaper proprietor, James Gordon Bennett.

All these races were for the type of car which would subsequently be available to the public; and nearly all of them were won by Panhards with the exception of the Paris-Vienna race of 1902. The result naturally was to boost the French industry above all others. De Dion had concentrated on small cars having engines of eight h.p. But from 1900 onwards he had a rival by the name of Renault. The Renault family owned a firm making buttons and linen amongst other things, but Louis and Marcel Renault were fanatically interested in the new cars. Using a Daimler engine they constructed another small car of eight h.p. with which they ended the De Dion and Panhard supremacy in light car racing in 1901.

Interest was at once aroused when Louis Renault finished eighth in the great Paris-Berlin race of 1901 against Panhards, Mors, the German Daimlers, and a host of other cars, a notable performance for an eight h.p. against the 40 and 60 h.p. of its rivals. But sensation

Preceding pages: In 1901 the automobile world was shaken
by the sudden appearance of a new type of car from the
German Daimler factory. This was due to a man called Emil
Jellinek (left), who had shown a great interest in Daimlers,
but had disliked the former models. He offered to help
finance the design of a new model, and insisted that it was
called Mercedes, after his daughter. Sensational as the
first model was, it was overshadowed by this 1903 model.
Below: Felice Nazarro, one of the giants of early motor-racing
in his Fiat, winning the Emperor's cup in 1907.

34

Below: Though cars with steam engines were not a success in the early days, the American Stanley Steamer was still in production in 1920, and the photograph shows one of this date. The Stanley brothers built their first steamer in 1897, by 1899 they were making 200 cars a year. They then sold their business to the Locomobile Company, but soon regretted the sale of their brainchild. Two years later they were again making steam cars, having had to redesign the whole machine to circumvent the patents they had sold. These were so much better that the Locomobile Company soon discontinued making them. The Stanley Rocket, another steamer, broke five world records in 1906, doing 127.6 m.p.h.

was created when Marcel Renault actually won the Paris-Vienna race of 1902 with a 16 h.p. car against the 70 h.p. Panhards and all the other historic racing cars of the period. Renaults by the way, always had the row of radiator tubes on each side of their bonnet which was to be their identification mark for years to come. Then in that fatal race, the Paris-Madrid of 1903, Marcel Renault struck a concealed drain in the verge of the road while overtaking Théry's Decauville, crashed, and was killed. But Louis carried on to full success as a manufacturer, though he never forgot his brother's death.

In the United States the American Times-Herald, owned by James Gordon Bennett, organized a much more scientific test for the new vehicles from 2nd November to 28th November, 1895, a test in which speed alone did not play the principal part but reliability did. In this trial it is amusing to note that horse power was tested by a machine, and the figure for the Duryea was 0.7 h.p. while the Macy registered the highest power, 2.5 h.p.

Racing at this time was beginning to have a direct effect on design. For example, tiller-steering was abandoned almost at once for the steering-wheel, resulting from the number of accidents caused by this unwieldy method of steering. Pneumatic tyres became essential and so on.

In all countries the idea that the car should travel at the pace of a horse vehicle was soon forgotten. But speed apart it was becoming necessary to think of more protection for the passengers and driver. At a low speed, not exceeding 13 m.p.h. or at most 20 m.p.h., anyone who grumbled because they were getting wet when it rained was told to use an umbrella. But the umbrella of the time was a substantial affair not unlike a parachute and often behaving like one, until it turned inside out. The he-man at the wheel was soon provided with a long, cone-shaped, waterproof garment with rubber seals at the neck and wrists, a garment called a 'Poncho' of which owners were inordinately proud, and though the very devil to get into, this coat was extremely efficient. Further, it was the outward and

Top: The 3½ h.p. Fiat of 1900. In general use by now were pneumatic tyres, which make the little car much more attractive.
Centre: Astonishing as it may seem, some early cars did venture far and wide. Charles Glidden and his wife, started in 1901 driving round the world in a Napier, and were still going strong in 1909. They covered 46,528 miles in 39 countries, driving from Australia to the Arctic Circle, Mexico to the Middle East, and if roads were impassable he fitted locomotive wheels and drove along railway tracks.
Bottom: A Pierce Arrow of 1906. Note that the treads of the tyres consist of the words 'non skid'.

visible sign that a man drove a car. Add a cloth cap worn peak behind, large crude goggles and leather gauntlets and you had the complete outfit.

Since no screens were provided, the driving compartment had no doors and no one had even thought of heaters, some protection for winter driving had also to be acquired. That 'protection' was a coat of goatskin worn hair outside, and still bearing traces of its original owner to those with delicate nostrils. Rich men however could afford genuine bearskin coats.

All this was very fine and rigorous, but more complications arose when the female passenger had to be considered. Women themselves did not drive at that time mainly because engines had to be started with a handle, which required very considerable muscular effort, apart from the necessity of knowing the car's mechanism thoroughly. The trouble was that the female of the period looked extremely attractive, as in all ages, but she *would* wear long, wide skirts, a great deal of frippery unsuitable for travel at speed, and an enormous hat which was usually decorated with a flower garden in full bloom. This was all very well for those stately runs round the park on a Sunday, taken in order to create black envy in every woman friend. But it was quite impossible on the open road. So, she was eventually persuaded to adopt a smaller hat with a veil extending down over her face but with a celluloid panel through which she could see and be seen.

By 1902 it was still not unusual to have a professional driver for what could still be called Society cars, a man specially trained and wearing the livery of horse-carriage days. But gradually even this relic of feudal times was replaced by serviceable leather. Incidentally, these drivers were called 'chauffeurs' – a strange gallicism, because chauffeur meant a man who fed the furnace of a steam engine.

All this masculine splendour was very fine so long as the car behaved, and by 1904 it still did not. Since everyone was learning the hard way apparently inexplicable troubles arose from the ignition, the carburetters, or even the valve gear, at the most awkward moments. In addition the untarred roads were not in the best of condition, and nails lost from horses' shoes frequently punctured tyres. To reduce the number of punctures cars were sometimes provided with a very curious affair shown on page 37. A piece of light steel cut into bars was held by a spring at one end and a cord at the other so that it just cleared the tread of the tyre. The idea behind this was that a nail picked up by the tread would not go right through to the inner tube until the tyre had

Below: A Daimler of the turn of the century with a 'tonneau' body, thus called because the backs of the rear seats resembled half casks to humorists. This car is said to have belonged to King Edward VII, who was a most enthusiastic motorist, and who contributed a lot to making motoring fashionable in England.

Top: This curious steel device became popular as a means of extracting nails from tyre treads. Punctures were very frequent in the early days because the roads were often strewn with nails which had fallen from horseshoes.

made a complete revolution. So this device was placed to catch and extract a nail as it went up from the ground in the tread.

All these troubles often meant a long struggle with oily machinery, much lying under the car to get at things and general exasperation. There were no garages or service stations, no easy source for spare parts other than the factory, no professional help at all. There were not even petrol stations handily placed. Every car carried one or more cans filled with petrol and other cans containing spare oil. To women this was all the more infuriating because car-owners were insanely enthusiastic about their machinery, so much so that the slightest irregularity in the engine, or car, meant an opportunity to waste hours pulling things to pieces, often in some quite desolate spot. Even if the car ran well there was still the discomfort caused by the clouds of dust which followed each car and penetrated everything.

It is necessary to understand all this to see why designers were at last forced to pay more attention to com-

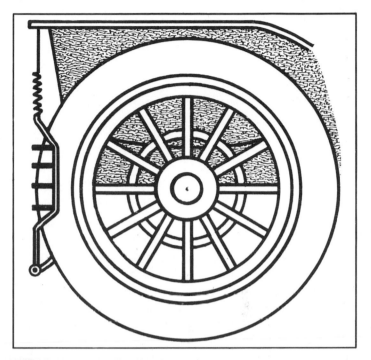

Below: A Daimler of the turn of the century with a 'tonneau' body, thus called because the backs of the rear seats resembled half casks to humorists. This car is said to have belonged to King Edward VII, who was a most enthusiastic motorist, and who contributed a lot to making motoring fashionable in England.

37

Marcel Renault at speed in the Paris-Madrid of 1903. This race was disastrous from the start, because of the terrific speed of the cars, the clouds of choking dust which the cars stirred up and the stupidity of the spectators themselves, who watched the race on the road. While attempting to overtake another car, which he could only barely perceive in the dust, Renault hit a drain shortly after this photograph was taken. The Renault somersaulted in the air and he was killed. This was the last race to be run on unguarded road. Many famous drivers and spectators were killed, and all the cars were stopped at Bordeaux, and returned to Paris by train.

fort for the car's occupants, and in this they were aided by the fact that Society could now accept a covered car for personal use, even if the majority of people thought of motoring as a he-man's exercise. But as yet there was no 'family' motoring worth recounting. Cars were mainly used for short pleasure trips and only rarely for holidays to some distant place.

All the same, Panhard had built several cars with closed bodies by 1902 as had De Dietrich. Panhard were responsible in 1904 for an extraordinary type of car which appeared to consist of the body of a horse-drawn 'Hansom' put on the back of a sternly mechanical chassis. The body was entirely the affair of coach-building firms at this time, as far as most car manufacturers were concerned. The engineering department still did not design the car chassis in conjunction with the body. The two design departments could never agree about anything, and this was further aggravated by coachbuilders still thinking in terms of a horse-carriage type of body.

Some of the French cars had heavy leather hoods which could be extended to protect the passengers in the rear seats, but the driver was still out in the open. Moreover these hoods were in effect a leather bag propelled mouth forward which became extremely troublesome in a high wind. As another concession to the weak De Dion fitted a wooden roof decorated round the edge with tassels, but it had no side protection.

Then in 1902 someone had a brilliant idea. In Africa horse-drawn vehicles were provided with a fabric contraption which could either be folded behind the seat or extended over it. This was in fact a protection against the burning hot sun but it could be adapted as protection against rain. So it was that the 'Cape Cart' hood was adopted for cars. At first it was a clumsy affair taking two men to erect or stow. The fabric tore easily, the 'sticks' which formed the support had a will of their own, and the whole contraption could be blown right out of the car, if someone forgot to tighten the front leather straps, which held the hood in position. In a sudden storm no one could be more unpopular than the driver who tried to erect this type of hood single-handed, while his girlfriend became wet to the skin.

At this time there was no provision for carrying luggage. You could, it is true, have a long basketwork-trough, mounted on the top of each rear mudguard, but that was chiefly for umbrellas. The basket did not get in the way, because the entry door for the rear seats was at the rear and not at the side. Originally ordinary oil lamps had been provided which were very troublesome.

This is the first Mercedes, into which Herr Jellinek put his money, the 35 h.p. Mercedes of 1901, and it created a sensation when it first appeared, because of its obvious advance in design. The next step in design gave this car the radiator which was to be the hallmark of Mercedes right up to the present day.

About 1904 it became possible to obtain great big brass headlamps using acetylene gas, a change made necessary by the all-round increase in speed. There was no dazzle problem in those days for there were not enough cars on the road to matter.

All this time speed was limited drastically in Britain to 14 m.p.h. by that law of 1896. Authority turned a 'blind eye' to speed as a whole it is true, but the situation was difficult, especially as anti-motorists were still numerous, and insistent that the law must be obeyed. Eventually Mr. Scott-Montagu, afterwards Lord Montagu, succeeded in persuading the British Parliament to pass a law making the registration of all cars necessary, with a promise that the speed limit would be raised. So it was that the Motor Car Act of 1903 set the limit at 20 m.p.h. and made a driving licence necessary, costing 5s. Registration entailed number plates, an idea which created a storm of protest. No gentleman, it was argued, would submit to having his private carriage fitted with large number plates. But, like all excitements of this character, the opposition faded away. This, by the way, was the first British law in which the phrase 'Motor Car' was substituted for 'Light Locomotive'.

In France speed was regarded with favour, though limits might be set through villages and cities. In Germany it was the same, with the result that car manufac-

ture in both countries progressed with greater speed than in Britain. By 1903 it was obvious that some kind of liaison between car engineers and coachbuilders would have to come. Centuries of experience had made the British coachbuilders famous. True they might not have the sense of line and beauty which made French coachwork different from all others, nor the strict regard for weight reduction obvious in the United States. But for sheer, solid, good workmanship the British could not be beaten.

Unfortunately the standards set them by the horse-carriage age were maintained with almost religious fervour. A body was usually constructed of a wood frame and wood panels by craftsmen accustomed to unhurried work and the individual requirements of customers. When completed the body was given several coats of paint by hand with brushes, and each coat was rubbed down until smooth before the final colour was put on. To complete the job a coat of varnish gave a mirror-like surface to the whole. It is easy to imagine how long this took but the future owner just had to wait. Even mounting the body on the car chassis had to be carried out with care, lest scratches might mar the surface paint. Maybe the result was magnificent, but it was not entirely suitable for a car which was to travel over dusty roads at speeds unknown in the horse age.

It may be difficult for people of today, accustomed
to giant presses and full mechanization, to realize that
this was typical of car production in 1900. The picture
shows the blacksmith's 'shop' in the Daimler works at
Coventry. Blacksmiths then made the parts for cars and were
often contemptuous of the new breed of 'engineers'.

By 1905 the frames of cars were beginning to be made
of steel instead of wood reinforced by steel, and were
much longer than previously. All the holes for the engine, gearbox, steering and other components were
marked off and drilled by hand, the engine and gearbox
being assembled in another section of the works. Big-end
and crankshaft bearings were hand-fitted, which was
quite an art in itself. Much time was spent making sure
that the engine and gearbox were properly in line before
the holding-down bolts were inserted. Even the brackets
for the springs had to be fitted to the spring eyes, an
operation involving more than an hour's work with
chisel and hammer.

Cars were now driven by chains and each chain had
to be cut to length, while the sprockets were marked off
and drilled for the retaining bolts. The same process was
necessary for the steering-gear, the radiator, fuel tank,
and what was called the 'dashboard' – the partition between engine and driving compartment, the term being a
relic of horse-carriage days. Tinsmiths made the bonnet,
coppersmiths the inlet pipe and fuel pipes. There was no
planned system for the assembly of the car, each gang
of fitters doing the work their own way. When the chassis was fully assembled it was usual for it to be 'signed'
by the men who had done the work. With a rough seat
fitted, that chassis would then be driven a number of

miles by one of the testers to check the completed whole.
Then the body had to be mounted.

Since the car frame was now longer the body designers had a much better chance to show their art, and
the result was a notable improvement in the lines of the
1904 cars, a definite elegance they had never possessed
before, which was all to the good. But the main trouble
was that the steel frame flexed considerably while the
car was running, which had a very bad effect on a body
intended to remain rigid. Also access to the machinery
was difficult, except to the engine which was outside the
body altogether. Sometimes trapdoors were cut in the
body floor, but some designers overcame the difficulty
by hinging the body at the back and bolting it down
in front, so that it could be raised to leave the chassis
bare. This served its purpose admirably but did not allow the body to be held firmly to the frame. In consequence the provision of a saloon, or Brougham-type body
was quite full of problems.

Panhard and British Daimler owned coachwork shops
of their own, though many cars had bodies specially
produced by order of the customer in specialist coachbuilder's works. The British Daimler, incidentally, had
a Frenchman, called M. Charles, in charge of their
body department, and the famous firm of Kellners
and Rothschild in France managed to construct several

It took the combined effort of Charles S. Rolls (left), aristocrat and fervent enthusiast, and Henry Royce (right), a sturdily independent engineer, to create this car, the Rolls-Royce, the reputation of which has never been equalled throughout the world to this day. Rolls, the enthusiast, is reputed to have said the following words to Royce, the brilliant engineer, when they agreed to form the company.

You make the cars, I'll sell them,

and we'll call it the Rolls-Royce

excellent closed bodies for Renault, Panhard and the German Daimler as early as 1902.

The fact that engines were becoming more and more powerful also gave coachbuilders more scope, even though the four-cylinder engines of the period would be regarded as rough today and they developed considerable vibration when used at full power.

But the sensation of this period, was provided by the German Daimler and it was a sensation everyone interested in cars at that time will never forget. A very rich Austro-Hungarian consul, Emil Jellinek, impressed by the performance of Daimlers in competitions, invested large sums in the firm. Possibly he was interested also because Kaiser Wilhelm of Germany was enthusiastic about the German Daimler cars. In 1900 Daimlers had produced a big, heavy-looking machine with no less than 30 h.p., identified by a large cellular radiator, hung low between the front ends of the frame. Daimler's engineer assistant Wilhelm Maybach, urged on by Jel-

44

Left: The first Rolls-Royce factory was situated at the end of this street in Manchester.

Right: The ordered chaos inside these premises. The workmen were chosen with extreme care, and were often supervised by Henry Royce himself. Royce was a stern taskmaster, and his men were kept constantly alert by his ability to spot the most minor of errors.

linek, set about the design of an entirely new car which appeared in 1901.

The new design created immediate interest with its two pairs of cylinders, its unusual system for governing engine speed, its simple type of magneto ignition, its raked steering column (in contrast to the nearly vertical column normal at the time) and its lines much finer than anything built previously. In addition it had a new form of gear control.

One of the principal difficulties for a driver during this period was the quadrant over which the gear lever moved. This was in one line, the position for each gear being marked by notches into which a spring loaded pawl fell to keep the lever in position. The driver raised this pawl by a trigger then had to feel for the next notch on the quadrant. If the car had to be stopped while top gear was engaged, the driver had to go through all the gears to obtain neutral or all but one to mesh first. Obviously it was extremely easy to make a mistake.

This was not possible with the new gear control. The quadrant was in the form of an H. When the lever was in the centre of the H no gear was engaged. By moving the lever sideways and backward first gear was meshed, for second the lever would be moved straight forward, then, for the third, moved back, sideways through the centre, then back again. Finally the lever was moved straight forward for top gear. Each gear movement ended positively. For reverse there was a separate lever. From then onwards every designer adopted the new arrangement for the gear quadrant, and so we came by the system used today.

To stimulate interest further the new car was called a 'Mercedes' not a Daimler. Mercedes was the name of Jellinck's eldest daughter, and was used partly to acknowledge his great financial help, partly to offset a dislike of things German still noticeable in France.

But sensational as this car proved it was overshadowed by the Mercedes of 1903. This machine had far better

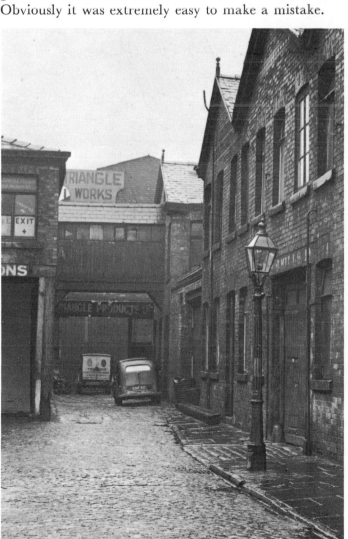

lines, was elegant, attractive, and absolutely novel–characteristics which influenced the whole world of car construction and all owners of cars. The old heavy-looking radiator was replaced by one simpler forming the front of the bonnet, the body was even more attractive, even the two levers one for the gear control the other for the hand brake, seemed right when mounted side by side on the off-side of the driving compartment.

The shape and design of every car was influenced by the new Mercedes, including the later American cars Pope-Toledo, Locomobile, and the like. Even the new big Italian Fiats, were difficult to distinguish from the Mercedes at first glance.

There were, of course, firms which deliberately ignored the new fashion and continued on their way maintaining the character of their cars on their own lines. Renault, for example, still held to their sloping bonnet with radiator tubes on each side of it. The British Daimler mounted the radiator in front of the car's bonnet but kept the characteristic finned top tank, the relic of which is visible in the small ridges on the radiator shell top of the modern Daimler.

Daimler had departed entirely from the German Daimler design by 1904 and was the premier British firm and proud of it. They were slightly contemptuous of

other people's ideas, but doing well and producing some thirty cars a week in the season. But even they were badly shaken in 1903 by the appearance of the first six-cylinder Napier, a car totally different from the four-cylinder models with which the firm had commenced business. Montague Napier was an engineer of note, grandson of the founder of D. Napier & Sons who had made coin weighing machinery since 1870. Napier had been a keen cyclist which had brought him in touch with a vigorous character, Selwyn F. Edge. Edge was passionately keen on the new motor cars, and the result was that Napier designed a British car following Edge's advice, the first of which ran in 1899 and that in turn led to the first six-cylinder Napiers of 1903. But Napiers might not have come to the fore so successfully or so quickly had it not been for Edge, who possessed in full measure that flare for publicity which people think is entirely modern. Edge saw to it that the Napier was always in the news. Whenever there was nothing special to give the Press, Edge always commenced a vigorous and argumentative correspondence in any paper which fell for his ideas. And the Napier sales increased rapidly.

To add to Daimler's troubles a totally new make of car appeared in 1904 designed by Henry Royce, a two-cylinder, 10 h.p. car, with three speeds. But this was followed by a much better four-cylinder 20 h.p. car in 1905, the result of Charles S. Rolls, an extremely enthusiastic and titled racing driver, son of Lord Llangattock of Monmouth, joining with Royce to give practical and experienced advice. That did not rival Daimlers for the moment but worse was to follow.

Firstly it was obvious that the men behind the new Rolls-Royce were thinking differently, thinking of a car which would be quiet, easy to drive, looked aristocratic, and was made as well as British craftsmen could contrive. Secondly the Daimler 'intelligence' section were sure that Rolls-Royce were experimenting with a six-cylinder engine and something 'odd'. The something 'odd' appeared in 1905, a strange, quite individual type of car called the 'Legalimit'. This car Rolls-Royce intended should be able to hold the legal limit of 20 m.p.h. anywhere along a normal main road whether flat or hilly, hence the name. That it had an eight-cylinder, 3½-litre, V engine was a distinct shock to everyone, the V engine being adopted so that the bonnet could be very low and inconspicuous compared with that of a normal car.

It was not a success but that did not lessen the shock. This car was definitely more silent than almost every other car, particularly at low engine speeds, a character-

istic its designers had sought in order to rival the small electric cars then being used for gentle ambles round Hyde Park on a Sunday by British Society.

Other British cars of note at that time were, the Wolseley, controlled by Herbert Austin, which had grown into a big car, always with a horizontal engine but with as much as 24 h.p. for one model. Herbert Austin had brought out the Wolseley 7½ h.p., open two-seater in 1903 at a time when vigorous argument was in full spate as to whether horizontal engines were to continue, or whether it was better to conform with the majority by going over to a vertical engine, whatever its type. Noisy with its single-cylinder engine, chain drive to gearbox and rear axle, this car did fill a gap in the market however. Maybe it was not as reliable as it might have been but it was popular nonetheless, as was its counterpart the so-called Siddeley, built in the same works with the same chassis but with a vertical engine. Wolseleys could always be distinguished by the gilled tubes for the radiator which were carried round to form three sides of what would have been the bonnet of an ordinary car. The Scottish Argyll was made from 1902 by the Hozier Engineering Co. of Glasgow who were general engineers. The pity of it is, the car section became the Argyll Motor Company which built for itself palatial offices, far more expensive than they need have been, while less consideration seems to have been given to the actual works. And the First World War put an end to this promising car in any case. Ignoring the new fashion Argylls continued with a radiator which also formed the front and sides of the bonnet. The Argyll also had a 'gate' quadrant for the gear lever every bit as good as that of the Mercedes, the only difference being that in the Argyll version the lever moved outwards, then forward, then back.

Lanchester too persisted with an excellent two-cylinder 10 and 12 h.p. car from 1900, a car for which the gear change needed no skill, and the tiller-steering was safe and efficient, while the springing gave real comfort over the worst road surfaces. But the Lanchester not only was unconventional in almost every respect but looked so, with the result that the inevitable dislike of the unusual, innate in the British, resulted in the car failing to have the full success it deserved.

But still car manufacturers were not thinking of the car for the million. That it was impossible to do so in the circumstances was due to the fact that every car still needed a great deal of attention from its owner if it was to run without trouble. That entailed a knowledge of mechanism, even if the standard of knowledge might

Below: The A.C. car of 1921 was not only a well-shaped machine, but was one of the best of the post-war, light cars, and made its name in competitions. A.C. was one of the first cars to have aluminium engines, and some had their rear axles incorporating the gearbox.

Right: The most famous of all Morris cars, the Bullnose Cowley, so-called because of the distinctive shape of its radiator. It had always been William Morris' firm intention to provide a small reliable car for ordinary people at a low cost, and with this car he succeeded.

Top: By now the Fiat firm was premier in Italy. This picture of a 1904 Fiat demonstrates that its lines have been influenced by those of the 60 h.p. Mercedes.
Centre: A hardly recognizable Cadillac of 1903.
Bottom: A version of the eight h.p. Rover of about 1904, now with its necessary accessories. The hood is held by straps to the frame—it was only later that it was attached to the windscreen. A feature of the design was that the engine and gearbox were held, almost as a unit, by one light alloy cradle. It was specifically designed for sale at low cost.

be low. So it was that technical know-how which was being accumulated with the expensive cars of this period, eventually made a popular car possible.

By 1906 however it was obvious that a closed car must be included in a manufacturer's range. The bodies were still the responsibility of the specialist coachbuilders, but that did not mean that the car manufacturer could ignore their special requirements any longer.

Some excellent Landau-type bodies appeared on Panhards. Renault offered other good closed bodies and were taking an interest in their manufacture in the car works. Mercedes too were to be seen with closed bodies. Daimler, British Daimler that is, produced a number, several of which were genuine saloons with the front passenger and driver under cover.

Over in the United States, though we did not realize it at the time, the car industry was thinking much more about a popular car, the car for ordinary people. That was the reason why so many of the early cars built by American manufacturers, afterwards to become famous, seemed so light, small and sketchy. Locomobile, for example, had produced a neat but small, two-seater, open-bodied runabout by 1900 and it had a steam engine. Stanley had a similar small car by 1901. Extraordinary as it may sound, Cadillac, later famous all over the world for luxurious, expensive cars for millionaires, commenced business producing a very small runabout with a single-cylinder engine astern.

A good example of the very light American car built at low cost in 1903-4 was the latest model Duryea. With the three-cylinder, 10 h.p. engine set transversely across the rear the car was very much open, though a hood was provided for the rear passengers. Four people could be carried, the driver and one passenger being in front, the remaining two higher up at the rear. It is interesting too that the Duryea advertisements of that year laid stress on elegance, comfort, simplicity, and silent running, not on speed, and also vouched for the machine as a 'Ladies' car, – the cost was £295.

These small, sketchy cars were regarded with some amusement by other American manufacturers, Christie, Haynes, Thomas, Pope-Toledo, Winton, and the rest, whose cars were on European lines – large, formidable and expensive – but the lighter cars were a step in the right direction. Moreover, even the large cars were being designed with more rational ideas of cost than those in Europe. More thought was given to their being bought by people who had very little interest in mechanics but who needed a vehicle merely for transport.

But there were engineers in Europe who thought that

THE 8 H.P. TWO-SEATED ROVER CAR. WITH CANOPY.

PRICE (Canopy and Lamps extra) - - - - £200.

Top: A Mercedes of 1902. Its immediate successor was the famous '60' Mercedes, with the now traditional radiator. Owners took great pride in the enormous, acetylene, polished brass headlamps. Behind the rear tyre can be seen a nail-extractor, a drawing of which is on page 37.

Bottom left: An Oldsmobile of 1900—a very popular car because of its quiet running and comfort.
Bottom right: The fashions of yesterday always seem ludricous to the people of today. But in fact the motoring gear of that age was most attractive, moreover sensible.

OLDSMOBILE CURVED DASH RUNABOUT
BUILT FROM 1900 THROUGH 1904

SPECIFICATIONS

CAPACITY -- Two passengers.
WHEEL BASE -- 66 inches.
TREAD -- 55 inches.
FRAME -- Angle steel.
SPRINGS -- Oldsmobile side springs.
WHEELS -- 28-inch wood artillery.
TIRES -- 3-inch detachable.
MOTOR -- 5 x 6-inch 7 H. P. horizontal.
TRANSMISSION -- All-spur gear, two speeds forward and reverse.
FINISH -- Black with red trimming.

EQUIPMENT -- Complete set of tools and pair of large brass side lamps.
RADIATOR -- Copper disk.
CARBURETOR -- Oldsmobile.
IGNITION -- Jump spark.
STEERING GEAR -- Tiller.
DIFFERENTIAL -- Bevel-gear type.
BRAKES -- Differential and rear wheel.
WATER CAPACITY -- Five gallons.
CIRCULATION -- Gear pump.
GASOLINE CAPACITY -- Five gallons.

BURBERRY
DUST WRAPPER

Below: Walter Owen Bentley, with his brother, had held the concession for the sale of the French car, the D.F.P. For a few years the Bentley brothers had a moderate success selling and racing them until Walter had the idea of making pistons of aluminium, and putting them into his racing D.F.P., with exciting results. He started to design his own car; by 1919 he had a chassis to show for his efforts, and in 1921 the first three litre Bentley was delivered to a customer. Almost instantly the name Bentley became synonymous with all that was smart and sporting in cars. This 4½-litre, supercharged Bentley, of 1928, was a very popular model.

Left: The smaller Morris Bullnose. This car served its public splendidly during the 1920s, and was one of the very first machines to be produced in quantity in Britain. *Right*: Another world-famous, small car, the Austin Seven, which was to remain Herbert Austin's particular pet throughout its long career. So popular was this car that many coachbuilders designed special bodies for the little machine, this one being the Gordon England Austin Seven.

During the first decade of this century it was quite usual for a manufacturer or sales agent to organize special long-distance runs, as publicity for his cars. These Oldsmobile runabouts are lined up in New York for the first trans-continental automobile race in 1905. The destination was Portland, Oregon, and 4,000 miles of crude roads were ahead. 'Old Scout' (on the left), outraced 'Old Steady' (right), and arrived 44 days later.

a car for the less wealthy majority was possible, even if they did not yet consider family motoring.

De Dion had already made a name for their six and eight h.p. machines with a form of gear change needing no operational skill. This French firm also made a neat little machine, appealing more in its convenience, than its speed. One model of this car actually had a four-seater body, the front passengers being seated looking backwards, those at the rear forward. In another version the front passengers looked forward, but the driver and another pasenger were on the rear seat. These De Dions cost about £210, the Wolseleys for example, in England cost under £200, which was cheap, but still too expensive in those days for anyone but the rich.

The British Vauxhall, product of the Vauxhall Ironworks of London, also produced a small car in 1905 with three cylinders, Rover made their six h.p. the same year and Humber a car called a Humberette which was a packet of trouble, though amusing. Both Rover and Humber had been cycle manufacturers of note; the Humber cycles made at Beeston, Nottingham having a magnificent reputation.

It was during this period that our great handicap – dust – was dealt with at last. In the days of horse-coaches the road from London to Bath had been provided with water pumps for almost every two miles to allay the dust nuisance, but that was now impractical. At a conference in Geneva in 1902 a Monsieur Charbonnier of that city showed an experiment he had made with hot tar on a road, which impressed the British and French delegates. In the United States experiments were being conducted using oil instead of tar. Then Leo Strachey, Editor of the Spectator newspaper, paid for two miles of the Farnborough-Aldershot road to be treated with heavy oil. By 1904 John Scott-Montagu also was doing his best to find a solution to the dust problem by investigating every known chemical which might be of use and, for a time, advocated 'Westrumite' which was a patent oily substance, expensive but efficient. For a time tar was used, with unfortunate results in hot weather, then at long last the modern road surface impregnated with asphalt solved the difficulty. But that was in the years to come.

No one can deny the immense strides the world's car industry had made by 1906. Cars had developed from crude rivals to the horse and carriage and able to equal their performance, to big, exciting machines which could exceed 60 m.p.h. and which were a new form of transport altogether. True, the family car was not yet born but the ghost of the idea was there.

Top: A 1925 Austro-Daimler. As its name implies, this
was one of the offspring of the German Daimler. It very
soon moved away from the German design, and approached
more the sports car type of design.

Bottom: The M.G. (for Morris Garages) had been on the
scene since 1923, when Cecil Kimber modified a Morris
Cowley for competing in trials and rallies. Up to 1929
these M.Gs. were quite successful, medium-sized sporting
machines of about two litres, and this is a model of 1926.
However, even more popular were the Midgets which first
came out in 1929, and which were based at first on the
popular Morris Minors, with engines of only 847 c.c.

Right: Lancia Lambda. First produced in 1922 this car was
amazingly successful. It had a V four-cylinder engine,
a monocoque body, together with independent front
suspension. Tests in the Alps proved it had incredibly
good road-holding power, and from a technical point of
view, it anticipated the developments of the late
Twenties. It was in production until 1931.

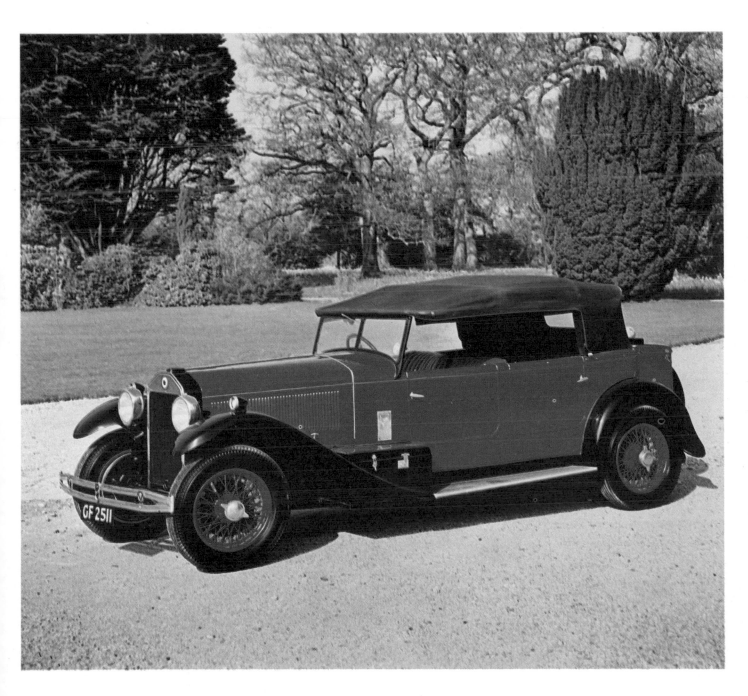

THROUGH MUD

AND DUST TO COMFORT

Preceding page left: The line-up of racing cars in a cloud of dust for a very early American Indianapolis race, on the specially-built, brick-surfaced track.
Preceding page right and this page below: As cars developed more graceful lines, it became fashionable for wealthy men to order incredibly elaborate interiors. This one was fitted to a Rolls-Royce, and was a masterpiece of the coachbuilder's art. The decor and furnishings were quite unsuitable for the dusty roads of the age, but nevertheless they carried a lot of prestige for the owner.

From 1906 to 1914 progress continued unabated. New models appeared at each year's Show, and new models, or new versions of older models were often announced any time the manufacturer pleased.

Two things were immediately apparent. Firstly, the cars were growing bigger and bigger, and more luxurious as a whole. Secondly, more and more accessories were announced and adopted. All this, in fact, assisted in the eventual production of the inexpensive family car, though no one would have thought so at the time. Motoring history makes it abundantly clear that luxurious equipment always appears first on the large, expensive type of car, then becomes available at far less cost for the popular machines that most people desire. Moreover motoring had how been accepted by society as far as Britain was concerned, and the car was taking the place of the horse and carriage finally and for ever.

The conversion was greatly assisted by the fact that royalty and leading citizens in every European country, as well as in the United States, were now driving cars. King Edward VII, even when Prince of Wales, was to be seen in a car whenever he could do so, and incidentally, could be encountered seated on a milestone cheerfully puffing a large cigar while waiting for his driver to remedy some defect in his quite splendid Mercedes. King Leopold II of the Belgians had a special body built for his car thereby creating a body type named 'Roi de Belges'. King Alphonso of Spain drove with verve at high speed, and not altogether with the approval of his ministers, who thought it undignified. William K. Vanderbilt Jr. not only raced with success but was definitely instrumental in assisting the growing American car industry to develop in every way he could. Count Louis Zborowski, the famous racing driver, always possessed the very latest Mercedes model and drove everywhere at fantastic speed, becoming a legend in his time.

Zborowski was a man who did much for the budding motor movement. Practically a millionaire from property owned in New York, he was of Polish descent but resident much of the time in France. Sad to relate he was killed during the 1903 hill climb on La Turbie hill, in the South of France, when driving the latest 60 h.p. Mercedes, because his shirt cuff caught in the hand throttle lever on the steering wheel and opened it full on a right-angle corner. His son Louis was equally enthusiastic and also became famous as a racing driver. Fate seemed to control the family for he too was killed in 1926 while racing, and for the benefit of the superstitious – was wearing the very cuff-links his father wore when the accident on La Turbie occurred.

Top: An extraordinary, six-cylinder, 120 h.p. Napier of 1908. The frame and body have been extended to provide extra seating for two more people. Thus eight people could travel in four rows of seats. The overall length was 21 feet, and it is probable that the frame bent before many miles had been covered.

Bottom: The Rolls-Royce Silver Ghost—the ultimate in elegance, and still considered so today. It was built in early 1907, and combined beauty with restrained aristocratic lines, which was a break with Rolls-Royce's former emphasis on power and strength. The wheel rims are detachable and the lamps are now electric.

63

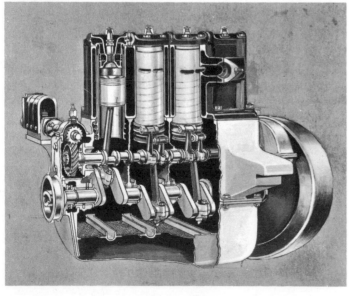

It is not surprising that emphasis on luxury now became a necessity. Without doubt the cars of 1906 were magnificent. The 28 h.p. Daimler gave a sense of immense power held in check, for example. The Panhards of that day were big, splendid machines. The German Mercedes became larger and larger, more and more formidable. In the States, the Locomobile, Matheson and Winton kept pace. The latest Italian Fiats seemed the embodiment of controlled power with from 80 to 100 h.p. available, and were a match in every way for their French or German rivals. Moreover the Fiat works had grown steadily by 1903 and, though they had the inevitable troubles, there was no doubt this firm was well on the road to success.

Naturally coachbuilders were encouraged to interest themselves chiefly in luxurious carriage bodies. One French Mors had a body fitted with the softest possible leather upholstery, hand-painted panels full of baroque cupids, a hand-painted ceiling, silver ashtrays, little vases for flowers, vanity mirrors, and thick fur carpets. Mind you the driver was still out in the cold, but that was of no importance, seeing that he was paid to be there and probably enjoyed it. Performance might suffer from the added weight, but that was of no consequence. These luxurious machines mainly came from France, for the French have a natural knack for making something both artistic and in good taste despite the ornamentation. By 1909 Eastern potentates had also realized the effect of magnificent cars as a demonstration of wealth – one of their cars had gold fittings, another even carried a gold throne.

It was not only the already established firms of the period which came to the forefront in all this. Distinctly to the annoyance of Daimler, Panhard, Fiat, and the other firms who considered with some justification that they were at the head of a national industry, Rolls-Royce were earning a reputation with altogether unexpected speed. By 1908, this Derby firm was doing exceptionally well with their 'Silver Ghost' model, which not only looked aristocratically different from all other cars but was noticeably silent and at its best when fitted with a first-class closed body. Rolls-Royce attained a great reputation in the East for this model almost immediately. It was Lord Montagu by the way, who suggested the beautiful little silver lady which has since graced that car's radiator.

Not without reason this period was to be known as the 'Golden Age' of motoring. It was also probably Rolls-Royce who set a new standard, by refusing to allow any body or accessory to be fitted to their cars which they

Top: By 1914 the Cadillac (this one is the Cadillac Landaulet) was regarded as the foremost luxury car in the United States, and deserved its reputation. It still holds this reputation today, and it is interesting to contrast this model with the gleaming chrome of the 1967 cars This 1914 model had a front seat wide enough to take three people in comfort on any journey even then.

Bottom: By 1914 the racing car was beginning to be a special machine, bearing little relation to the production model of that time. This is the French Delage, which the burly French driver, Rene Thomas, drove to victory in the 1914 Indianapolis 500 miles race.

Brooklands, which until the war was the English
sporting driver's mecca. This motor-racing track
irregular in shape, several miles around, and complete
with steep bankings, was built as early as 1907. Here
not only big powerful racing cars raced, but there were
also events for ordinary sports cars. It was this
race-track more than any other factor, which contributed
to the improvement of the performance of British cars.
During the race, thirty seconds after this picture was
taken in fact, the leading car, a Bentley, crashed at
130 m.p.h., killing its driver, Clive Dunfer.

considered unsuitable, whether the customer wanted it or not. They also set a new standard in demonstration, for their salesmen were past-masters of the art of displaying the car to full advantage, especially in top gear and for silent running.

It was this quest for silent flexibility which led British Daimlers into trouble. Charles Y. Knight of Wisconsin, America, had designed an engine with sleeve valves which slid up or down as required instead of the cam-operated 'poppett' valves used almost universally. In 1908 Daimlers acquired the rights to manufacture this engine and did so, though the result was a sleeve valve engine of their own design working on the Knight principle. Certainly the new engine was silent... but the cold of winter and consequent lubrication troubles generally made sleeve valve engines very difficult to start of a morning, and eventually they were abandoned.

But, as far as British cars were concerned, something else had a profound influence on design, an influence which was to assist materially in the future production of the kind of car in which you and I are interested.

A wealthy Weybridge resident, Mr. H. F. Locke King, who had driven his big Italian Itala over long distances in Europe, was certain that the speed limit and other national restrictions had led to the performance of British cars lagging behind that of foreign cars, especially on long alpine climbs. So during 1906 and 1907 he built at Weybridge the big banked track which we all know as Brooklands, a track on which speed was unlimited. He became at once the most disliked citizen in Weybridge on account of the noise, bustle and fumes. But on that track, engines developed fast until even an engine of 1500 c.c., small by the standard of that era, could develop as much as 50 h.p.

Naturally S. F. Edge of Napiers saw the opportunities at once, and the track commenced business on 28th June, 1907, when he drove a 60 h.p., six-cylinder Napier single-handed for a world twenty-four hour record, accompanied by two other similar Napiers, each driven by two of the company's drivers. The attempt was entirely successful and the publicity Napiers gained in this venture boosted sales considerably.

Below: This Peugeot Bébé was produced in 1913, just when interest was returning to the small car, which was economical to run and maintain, and it proved most successful. Rated as six h.p. the Bébé had a four-cylinder engine, whereas many of the rival small cars were provided with only two cylinders.

Day in, day out, after that experiment, cars and all aspects of their mechanism were tested on Brooklands, with the result that the performance of the British car improved beyond all expectations.

Racing as a whole though was not quite as useful as it had been, largely because the racing cars were being built more and more to a specialized design, and were becoming less and less connected with the sort of cars people could afford. Moreover the frightful disasters of the 1903 Paris-Madrid race over ordinary roads crowded with spectators and obscured by immense clouds of dust had stopped road-racing as such for good. From now onwards all future races were to take place on heavily-guarded, short circuits.

But even so there were some benefits. For example the race for the French Grand Prix in 1906 was won by a huge Renault largely because it was fitted with detachable rims for its wheels. Instead therefore of levering off a burst, or punctured tyre, replacing it with another and inflating the new tyre, all the driver and mechanic had to do was to undo a ring of nuts, take off the rim

and tyre, replace it with a new one, and continue. So obviously successful was this that the idea was rapidly adopted for normal cars and one more handicap for ordinary drivers disappeared. Prior to this, there had been a strange attempt to solve the problem by providing a rim and tyre with clips, called a Stepney wheel, which could be bolted on to the rim of the car's ordinary wheel if a puncture occurred. But this was an operation needing more care than the ordinary driver was likely to exercise. However, it took a lot of careful publicity before people were convinced that these new detachable rims were safe at any speed.

But that was not the end of the matter. During 1907 and 1908 wire wheels became more and more usual, that is steel-spoked wheels like those of a bicycle. Rudge Whitworth, who manufactured most of these wheels, brought out a new method of attachment for them, which allowed the wheel and tyre to be removed very quickly by undoing the hub nut with a special spanner. This was an even faster process than using the detachable rim, though more frightening to the uninitiated. But

A fleet of 12 six-cylinder Napier cars outside the Imperial Institute in London. By command of King George V they were placed at the disposal of the Royal guests during their coronation visit in 1911.

gradually every racing car came to use these wheels and confidence was restored.

Curiously enough Brooklands racing also had an effect on coachbuilding, as soon as it was understood that a car could be forced through high wind or the air with more ease if it had a special 'streamlined' shape. Up to that time the accent had been on 'windcutting', i.e. providing the car with a sharp nose. Now it was proved that the stern end was the part which needed more attention. The result was that the redesigned bodies of British cars, plus the power gained from experience at Brooklands made the British car at last capable of rivalling the French in performance.

But performance apart, much was happening to the car itself. Definitely, if slowly, the more famous coachbuilders were moving away from the horse-carriage technique, and approaching a body to complement and withstand the performance of the car. True there were still many examples of luxurious bodies, magnificently built and equipped, but quite obviously designed with no regard to the chassis.

All the large manufacturers provided windscreens now, though this accessory might still be an extra. The screens were high, complicated, solidly built and glitter-ing with polished brass, but they were screens. Since the wiper was yet in the womb of time a section of the screen could be opened when it rained.

The shape of these bodies was beginning to change – there were even luggage carriers and valances to the much larger mudguards. Speedometers were available, again as extras; instruments were designed in a better shape and grouped in a more sensible arrangement. In 1908 it became possible to have a set of electric lamps instead of acetylene gas ones, which had been developing into near searchlights. Today British cars are usually provided with full lighting and engine-starting equipment by the world-famous firm of Joseph Lucas. The first electric lamps they supplied in 1908 were almost exact replicas of the old oil lamps and which in turn had been copied from those used on horse carriages. The Lucas catalogue of the same year gives £4. 10s. 6d. as the cost of a pair of brass lamps. They also list a conversion set to allow electric bulbs to be fitted inside oil lamps so that oil fuel could be used as a reserve. Dynamos had to be fitted wherever possible alongside the engine and in consequence were often driven by leather belts. Later, of course, provision for the dynamo was included in the engine design. Batteries were still very

tricky, it is true. Starters followed later, not yet as universal fittings but again as extras.

In all this the difference between American and European ideas was very marked. In America electric lights and a starter were considered far more important than in Europe, added to which the American bodies of the time were built not quite so much for magnificent appearance and attractive lines, as for comfort and low cost. The Americans had also built a speed track in 1911 at Indianapolis, which was designed for much higher speed than Brooklands. But it never had the same effect on design. By now, driving in the United States was also full of limitations and drivers were encountering the same problems as the British had had to face. The probable reason for this was that racing was regarded more as a spectacle, a circus appealing through its danger and not as an exercise for determining which car was best. Packhard, Pierce-Arrow and Peerless were names in the headlines in the States at that time – the equivalent of Panhard, Peugeot, Fiat, Mercedes in Europe. But none was yet in the Rolls-Royce class.

From the commencement of the period the whole accent in Europe was on cars for the wealthy, cars which could be as thoroughly equipped as the mind of man

could then contrive. Below the surface, however, many were thinking that if a suitable utility car could only be designed, there was an immense demand. This idea was still only a dream, but the dream recurred.

And then, abruptly, a sensation. That difficult man, Henry Ford, suddenly produced the very car that the dreamers had dreamed of, but had never given practical consideration. And what a car it was! The first machines were presented to the amazed but interested public on 1st October, 1908, and were called the Ford 'Model T'.

The car seemed very light, very light indeed, even by the standards of the United States. With a four-cylinder engine of the simplest type, valves at the side, a detachable head, a crude looking carburetter, an extraordinary electrical generator combined with the engine flywheel, a planetary gearbox, the gear of which could be changed by pushing pedals – this seemed an astonishing car. All equipment was reduced to the minimum, the body was high, seated four, and had a cape hood. The drive was through a propeller shaft with one universal joint forward; and according to report, Henry Ford had said, 'You can have any colour provided it is black'. The critics, especially those in Europe, refused to take the Model T seriously. It was, they said, one

Left: Henry Ford, the man who stuck obstinately to his ideal of a car for all, and by dint of revolutionizing the car industry, produced it. Ford discarded all the long accepted methods of manufacture, and set his mind to producing millions of the same part at once. He is credited with the innovation of the assembly-line method of car production.

Right top: This 1908 Oldsmobile is at last showing a departure from a mechanical carriage, and is becoming an automobile in its own right. At this stage the usual building material for a car was still wood; poplar for sheathing, and ash for supporting members.

more example of Henry's irresponsibility, his non-conformity with accepted ideas.

All this may have seemed true to the rival manufacturers of the time. But the black Model T lived for 17 years, no less, and countless people were able at last to enjoy motoring who could not have done so without its help. The most important point was the price, 250 dollars, about £70, and that was justification enough.

Of course the car became the subject for every humourist. Volumes of jokes could be collected on the subject, jokes were even manufactured by Fords as good propaganda. Much of the humour centred round the fact that reverse, engaged by pushing a pedal as the gear was planetary, could be used as a really good brake while the car was going forward. If the driver continued to press the pedal after the car had stopped the Ford ran back. But there was no doubt whatever that the Model T was a godsend to vast numbers of people who could not afford any other car, and especially to people with families. Driven properly it was not only reliable, but quiet and reasonably comfortable. Driven badly it could give real trouble.

It is now estimated that 15 million Ford Model Ts were made – 15 million! Naturally there arose a most vigorous trade in improvements for the car, accessories, new cylinder heads, better brakes, and coachbuilders could provide saloon-type bodies to replace the sombre, workmanlike, but severely practical, open four-seater. However much an elaborate closed body might be out of place on the Ford many people naturally found it extremely useful. Henry Ford had indeed created the historic vehicle of the period.

As far as Europe was concerned though, some manufacturers were thinking of the same market but finding it difficult to determine what type of car would suit best. The principal difficulty was that a car for the ordinary family had to be inexpensive and ought to be a saloon. But to make a car inexpensive it had to be produced in thousands. In the United States, obviously, there was an immense home market. In Europe no one could see that quantity of customers, not even if export was taken into the account. It was also becoming apparent that the method of production which had served for so long would have to be reorganized. But the cost of the

machinery necessary for this seemed astronomical.

The Americans had solved this problem. Big presses to form body panels and other components very quickly were already in existence, while engineers were already planning for quantity production using machines rather than men – though this idea was still in its infancy. By 1914 the Americans had already produced bodies, and closed bodies at that, made chiefly by welding pressed-steel components together. The result might not seem to have the style considered essential in Europe, but to the Americans the main problem was to produce transport, not mechanical masterpieces, and transport for people who did not have a specialist driving skill.

Over here in Europe there suddenly seemed to be a spate of small two-seater, open cars, including a number which forcibly reminded veteran motorists of the chaos in design apparent when motoring had commenced. In France for example, a horrible belt-driven tandem-seated affair called a Bedellia appeared, a veritable 'Cycle-car' and all the worse for that. Equally startling but better, was the G.W.K, Grice-Wood Keiler, a two-cylinder, friction-driven, little car at £150, the per-formance of which was remarkably good provided the driver knew how to handle the mechanism. In contrast were the six h.p. Peugeot on more regular lines, the small Adler, and Wolseley 'Stellite' nine h.p. at £158. Another horror was the–four cylinder-engined Pilot which had a friction-drive guaranteed to give trouble.

But before these new small cars could settle down came the First World War. Thus ended a period unique in motoring history, a period when life was calm, very pleasant, not too noisy and to us of that era, secure. But a period when wealth was in the hands of the comparatively few. It was indeed a 'Golden Age' on which to look back, even allowing for the fact that everyone forgets troubles, and remembers only happiness. The war came and car manufacturing came to a standstill. Mechanized transport, however, had its uses, it appeared, even for war. Two cars which proved invaluable were the Ford Model T and the Rolls-Royce. The former effectively carried a machine gun with an armoured shield. The latter was used to carry a great weight of armour and machine guns for some of the time in the Western Desert.

Below: A 1929 Alfa Romeo. A.L.F.A. (Anonima Lombarda Fabbrica Automobili) built French Darracqs as far back as 1909. At the time of the First World War a young engineer named Nicola Romeo took over, added his name and called the outfit Alfa Romeo. It soon began to make its name known on the road-circuits and race tracks of Europe. This is the beautiful six-cylinder Gran Sport.

Top right: Another specialist version of the Austin Seven. This machine was provided with a much neater sports type of body and radiator shell, and was called the Austin Swallow. In this case, as in most of the others, the engine was tuned to give more power, and naturally all were dearer than the standard version.

Bottom: This Crossley-Burney of 1934 was a most interesting machine. These short-lived cars were originally conceived by Sir Dennis Burney, designer of the R 100 airship. The car as a whole was lighter than most at that time, had independent suspension, and the engine was designed by Crossley.

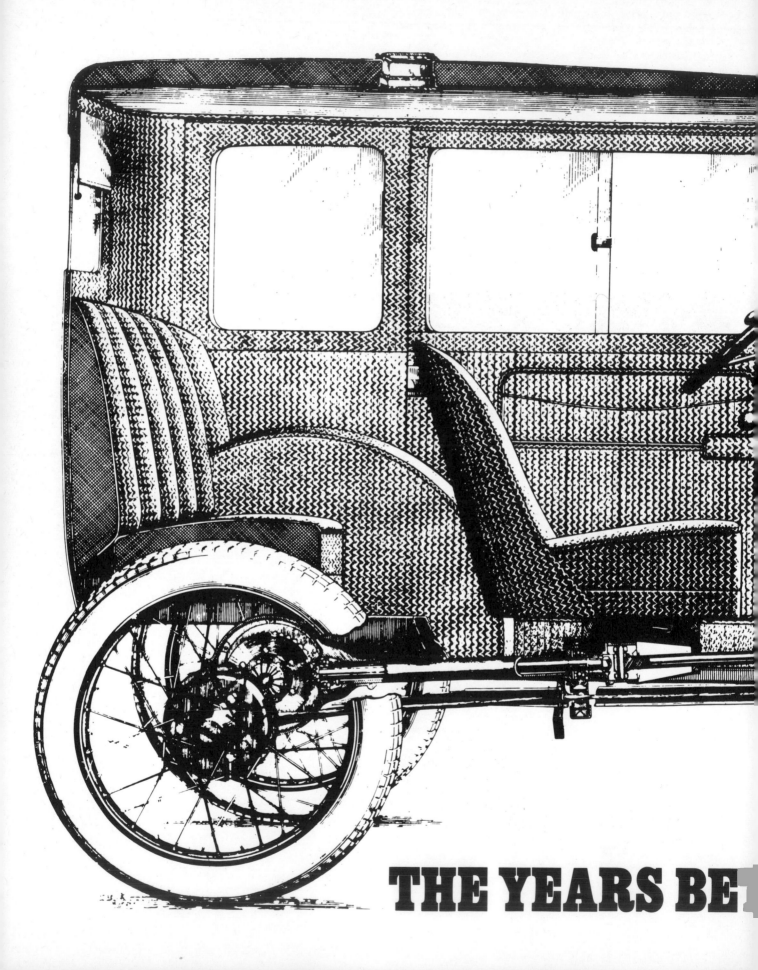

THE YEARS BE

WEEN THE WARS

After the First World War had ended, we entered a
new era and everything in Europe seemed radically
changed. All car manufacturers had learned a great
deal about production from the intense supplying of
war material. Time and Motion Study had ceased to
be a theory and had become a necessity.

But an even greater change was obvious. The desire
for motoring was no longer confined to those with
enthusiasm for mechanism because everyone wanted
cars. Now that engine starters were almost universal
and cars were becoming much more reliable, women
could drive – though men still affected a superiority
about the art.

The saloon car was far more popular though many
models still had open bodies. Cape hoods were neater,
much easier to erect and fold, there were even side
curtains which made the car reasonably waterproof
and did not blow away as their predecessors had.

Moreover there was even a traffic problem, largely because commercial vehicles were now in general use, and what had made an even greater difference, the government had removed the speed limit at last, ostensibly because the car had played so great a part in the war.

Because of all this the main problem before the design department of a manufacturer was to work out how to design the type of car the majority of people would buy, taking into account that although money was now spread more equally over the population, prices as a whole had risen, and, therefore, the ideal car would still have to be inexpensive.

The only possible solution was to lay out the works for production in quantity, and that meant acquiring extremely expensive machinery, and a new type of workman who could produce good cars at speed with less emphasis on loving craftsmanship. It also followed

After 1920 there suddenly appeared a spate of little cars with small engines. Violent controversy arose between enthusiasts over what to call them—Light Cars of Cycle Cars. These two cars are typical of them.
Top: The cheap and popular American Hupmobile.
Bottom: The English Stellite, produced by Wolseleys, though

that the type of car built would now have to appeal to a wider field, and exports were of paramount importance, since the war had depopulated most European countries, Britain in particular, and the market was not great enough at home to justify mass-production purely for one country's needs.

But if there is one characteristic which stands out when one is analysing the trend of the car industry it is unexpectedness; and this was amply demonstrated from 1920 onwards with a sudden spate of little cars with small engines. At first sight this might seem to be a case of misguided thinking, for it was obvious that this type of car would not appeal to the vast majority of people whatever its cost.

But there were more young enthusiasts than had been anticipated and they took to the new small cars as ducks to water. Violent argument arose over whether to call the machines 'cycle' cars or 'light' cars, which was vigorously encouraged and commented on by the newly created rival motoring magazines. Tempers rose to fever pitch and partisans became almost vitriolic in their support for the different cars.

At all events the cars were interesting. The G. N., a product of H. R. Godfrey and Frazer Nash, was a wire-wheeled two-seater with a fierce, two-cylinder, air-cooled engine and, of all things, belt drive. G.W.K. improved their friction gear, little two-cylinder, water-cooled car, and Granville Gradshaw was responsible for the A.B.C. – so called for no known reason. With two horizontal, air-cooled cylinders and a four-speed gearbox, an excellent gear control with the 'gate' placed vertically instead of horizontally, this car was very attractive. But it gave a great deal of trouble, firstly because its steel cylinders warped, secondly because the connecting rod roller-bearings did not last and thirdly because small parts continually went wrong. In addition Trojans produced an extraordinary vehicle with a two-stroke engine and solid tyres. This became famous for being able to tackle any gradient, though its speed was then reduced to that of a hearse.

By way of contrast there was an excellent little Singer, a big car in miniature, with a four-cylinder engine, expensive but remarkably reliable and reasonably comfortable. Prior to this Singer had been bicycle manufacturers in Coventry, and had then made motor cycles, one model of which was especially intriguing because it had its engine in the centre of an aluminium thick-spoked rear wheel.

Before the war a firm called A.C., of Thames Ditton, the initials standing for Auto-Carriers, had built three-

wheeler, two-seater, goods carriers, and now turned to more normal four-cylinder cars which, under the supervision of S.F. Edge, speedily acquired a fine reputation in a blaze of publicity. In addition Calthorpe and Calcott also entered the small car field; and then an Etonian enthusiast, Lionel Martin, produced the first Aston-Martin, Aston being a hill used for competitions in which the protoytpe had done well. That car too was expensive but it was definitely good and its subsequent history, except in finance, was full of successes. Another small car was the Lagonda, named by its sponsor Wilbur Gunn after a river in his own country, America. Originally his firm was concerned with steam launches on the Thames, then it began to build rather eccentric-looking, motor-cycle and fore-carriage combinations, notable for enormous C-shaped leaf springs. His first car was a little two-seater characterized by a 'bull-nosed' radiator which looked decidedly heavy. But those little cars were the ancestors of the big modern Lagondas for all that.

it bore none of the Wolseley distinctive features.

Top: A typical family saloon car of this period was the Rover shown here. Originally Rovers had been cycle-manufacturers, but by now they had achieved a reputation for providing good, sturdy, reliable cars. This model of 1930 has a Weymann body, and was called a Light Six Saloon.

Bottom: This Austin 12, four-cylinder car of 1922 was one of the most successful models ever to come from the Longbridge factory. Not only was it entirely dependable and durable, but it was sold at a particularly tempting price. It is probable that with this model the name of Austin first became universally known.

Below: A 1933 Fiat. By now the open car was almost out of fashion, and those few which were built had a more substantial hood, together with windows which could be lowered or at least removed. Moreover the accent was on cars for family use, as this Fiat shows. The bumper fitted was a real bumper, or buffers, held clear from the frame by spring arms.

Top right: An American supercharged Auburn of 1935. This car in fact exemplifies just how much it had developed along European lines.

Centre: An Armstrong-Siddeley. This was the first car for which a semi-automatic gear was provided in Britain.

Bottom: A 1921 Rolls-Royce. The Silver Ghost was made from 1907-1926, and went through several changes. It is amusing to note the little doormats incorporated into the running board, for the feet of the well-shod English gentry.

A Buick of 1919. William C. Durant of Buick had been
the prime mover in the formation of General Motors about
ten years before this, and since then had done much
towards its success. This sporty model is a two-seater.

On the continent the same trend towards small
two-seater, open cars was apparent. Ettore Bugatti
was responsible for a famous little car, the French
Salmson for another, and here belt-driven monstrosities
were not so usual. Unfortunately, from one point of
view, nearly all these manufacturers became entangled
with competition racing, and the result was that their
products gradually developed into sports-type cars,
which were less attractive to the mass of ordinary people
who were waiting for the genuine family car.

Competitive racing by now usually increased the
cost of cars unless expenditure was carefully watched.
But there was one advantage from this increased competition, it forced engineers to work day and night to
induce more power from their engines. Power was what
was wanted, and power from small engines. So the
1500 c.c. engine came to have over 50 h.p., and that
was to be of the utmost value in years to come for
a different type of car altogether.

But not every manufacturer was diverted into the
high performance sports car field for small cars. In
1922 the Austin 'Seven' appeared. Prior to this, Austin,
in the face of considerable opposition, had obstinately
refused to agree that there was anything wrong with
his horizontal engine, and the argument over this point
had led to his leaving Wolseleys and starting another
firm in his own name. The first small car to come from
this firm was the Seven. Austin had actually created
it himself, drawing the plans at his home, Lickey
Grange, and doing exactly what he wanted to do. Norm-
ally, heads of very large firms rough out an idea, then
have the real work of making the thing practical developed by the drawing office. But from the very beginning Austin had had the dream that a small car could

be built for the thousands of people who could not afford
motoring with the cars then on the market, and his
dream came true. One of the most successful cars ever
built, the 'Tiddler', as it was nicknamed almost immediately, sold in vast quantities for very many years,
and is still selling today, though at second hand.

What Austin made in 1922 was a car reduced in size
rather than a design based on the idea that it must be
small. The Seven had a quite normal four-cylinder
engine, the ordinary gearbox and final drive. Though
rated as seven h.p. the engine developed at least 10.
When the prototype machine was ready in the firm's
experimental shop it was Austin himself who took it
for its first run, and he did so alone. Moreover he
wore the familiar bowler hat which had become almost
a symbol to everyone in the works.

The original car was created by Austin as a legitimate
successor to his Wolseley six h.p. The modern version
of the 'Tiddler' which appeared in 1945 was called an
A 30, and had a larger engine, a different chassis and
much better equipment. But what developed in this car
has happened to every model which sells well as the
years go by.

The Seven flourished and many families started
their motoring with it. There was room for two in
front, room for the child, or dog, or luggage at the
rear. Before a year had elapsed saloon bodies could be
provided for the car, and that filled a definite want at
once. Accessories of every kind were marketed as well.
The Seven could not be called quiet, or very comfortably sprung, nor did it have much room for its
occupants, but it was very handy, very inexpensive to
run, cost at the works £165, and could be kept in the
garden shed.

Even Austin was surprised at the flood of subsequent
orders and it was this car which put the new firm in a
satisfactory financial position, thus allowing for greater
expansion. As further proof of their popularity Sevens
were built under licence too in the United States,
France and Germany.

When I took one of the first of these cars to the South
of France the proprietor of a large luxury hotel, the
courtyard of which was filled with big cars, was so
amused at the little machine that he insisted on putting
it in the wine cellar, and refused to charge garage for it.

William Morris was also pursuing his ideal of a car
for the million with his Morris Minor; but more about
him later. It was a well-built little replica of a large
open two-seater car, built at low cost; and it sold in
large quantities. Peugeot's earlier Bébé was a smaller,

A Citroën also of 1919. It is interesting to note that the Citroën still has solid disc wheels, whereas the Buick does not. This Citroën has an open body, which was still popular, partly because it cost less money, and Citroën always catered for those who could not afford the normal, large-engined car. Prior to manufacturing cars Citroën had been known as manufacturers of a special form of bevel gear. André Citroën first introduced Henry Ford's methods to the European car industry, and soon after the war he was engaged in mass-producing cars for the world.

A fine example of the magnificent Hispano-Suiza. This car, more than any other, epitomizes this early age of motoring. Coveted by all drivers, it was however very expensive. Even its styling implied its immense power, and its luxury and excellence was immediately apparent. This particular car was first owned by the famous racing-driver, Count Zborowski, and then by his great friend Clive Gallop, who is here seen at the wheel.

if amusing two-seater, in comparison, but it never became anything like as popular as its British rivals.

By and large, this period had much in common with the early pioneeering days as far as the more unusual of the small cars were concerned. There was the same enthusiasm not always properly directed, the same type of adventurous design, and the same striving with difficulties both technical and financial. But the more normal small cars were a further step in the right direction, towards the real family car of the future.

The war had had a different effect on other countries as far as car design was concerned, and the demand had changed according to a country's fortune in that war. Italy, for example, took a long time to recover and when this happened all cars were built with an eye to popular demand, most of them smaller than in the years before. Germany had more than enough trouble on her hands to make car production easy, but again the demand was for less expensive transport. It was obvious in Europe that the days of the big luxury car,

the car type of which we had all been so proud, had gone for the present and might not recur in the future.

In the United States, on the other hand there was no real demand for the very small car, but more insistence on a big car at lower cost. Nor was there a general desire for engines smaller in size than the large ones which had been regarded as typically American. The difference was caused, of course, mostly by the cost of fuel, which was lower in America than in any other country, so the desire for fuel economy which was

paramount in Europe since the war, did not exist in the States. The American car industry had benefitted naturally from being able to continue development for so long while Europe was at war, the result being that much lee-way had to be made up before the production methods of the two continents were on a par.

The most difficult part of car production was the body. In the United States manufacturers had had to face this difficulty, since a form of mass-production had been adopted in 1910, much earlier than in Europe. They too had found that a chassis lent itself admirably to the new method, but when it came to the body the shell might be built quickly by using huge presses, yet the time taken for final painting could not be cut, so long as men with brushes did the work. At least one firm made a most ingenious machine to roll paint on to the panels, another invented a machine using brushes, but it proved quite unreliable and exceedingly costly. Naturally it served no useful purpose to make chassis in thousands, and then have to keep them for weeks and weeks until the painters could catch up with the work. So it seemed like a miracle when someone conceived the idea that perhaps paint could be sprayed on to the panels.

The body made completely of steel instead of a frame with steel panels became practicable when the Dodge brothers of America were persuaded by the Budd Manufacturing Company that such bodies were not only possible but distinctly better for their cars. The result of this great step forward was that Dodge's car production reached one million by 1923.

In France Weymann produced an altogether new type of body which was to have a profound, if temporary, effect from 1923 onwards. Instead of steel panels the new design used leather or leather substitute stretched over a wood frame, the various members of which were not in actual contact wood to wood. It was claimed that under the new system a body took much less time to construct, while the minor squeaks which often resulted when the normal body had been stressed on a fast car, were eliminated. Unfortunately these benefits were off-set by the greatly increased cost, so the metal body won approval in the end.

But another version of the same idea carried out with less complication and at less expense proved of considerable value in providing saloon-type bodies for the less expensive cars, the Austin Seven and the Ford Model T for example, thus providing a machine much nearer to our ideal family car. That pleasant little car the Morris Bullnose which had appeared first just

Because of the increase in prices generally after the First World War, thousands could still not afford the type of car which had been produced up to this time. The growing need was met by smaller cars. Four which became well known are seen below, all sold most successfully and were very popular.

Below: An open-bodied Wolseley of 1924. By now the car had lost its individual frontal appearance, and was approaching the design which we know today. Both screen and hood are now much neater, and the spare wheel is mounted on the running-board, as there was no boot, and a luggage carrier was fitted to the rear.

before the war and was improving year by year, and the Oxford and the Cowley could also be seen with the same type of body, usually provided though by a specialist coachbuilder.

It was of the utmost importance that production costs themselves were kept as low as possible both in France and England. This was largely because it was still possible to buy an American, 20 h.p., four-seater car in Europe in 1922 for only about £250. Moreover it seemed quite apparent that the United States was concentrating not on performance, nor even on style, but on a

car for the ordinary family, and already they seemed to be succeeding without reducing the size or convenience of the machine. The Americans made some sound innovations too. Their cars now had the gear and hand-brake levers in the centre. The shock to enthusiasts when Rolls-Royce actually did the same in 1922 is still fresh in the memories of those who were in the industry at the time.

But it was abundantly apparent that the new lever position had advantages whichever side the driver sat, since the off-side doorway was freed from obstruction. There had been, in all countries, a temporary attempt to solve the problem by making the gear lever short and placing it on the steering column, and making the brake lever a handle projecting from the instrument board, but this was never really popular except with the Americans who persisted with the handle for the brake.

One of the most intriguing things about the earliest cars was that they all had right-hand drive, that is the driver sat on the right having the control levers outside the body on his right. But the European rule of the road being mostly 'keep right' this seemed extraordinary and

Left bottom: Herbert Austin's most famous model, the Austin Seven. This is the first, of 1922, of a long line of Austin Sevens. He designed it himself and took a fatherly interest in it all his life.
Below: The five h.p. Citroën of 1923, with a 'clover leaf' body. It had few accessories, as did most cars of

that time, was even austere, but all these cars were just what the world wanted.
Bottom right: The Ford Model T gave way to the Model A in 1928 after nearly 20 years of production, and this was made for four years. This is in fact the 1932 model, and has obviously developed into a sturdier car.

about as inconvenient as it could possibly be. Of course it was not long before the controls were altered to suit the rule of the road abroad, but the idea that major controls should be placed for the right hand of the driver resulted in all British cars continuing to have right-hand drive and right-hand levers for years.

Special contrivances to avoid dazzle were becoming very popular by 1925, some of them of extraordinary complication. In at least two of these devices a system of levers and rods enabled the driver to turn the whole headlight downwards while keeping the beam at full strength, which worked well until age and wear made the headlamps quite unsteady in any position. There were also ingenious shutters to open or close over the headlamp glass, screens lowered or raised over the lamp, and other devices innumerable. It is curious that we always commence with complication before simplicity is attained. The French and Americans however soon adopted out-of-focus bulbs which reduced the strength of the lights at need and turned the beam downwards, an idea which led to the lighting system of today with two filaments in one bulb.

One great step forward was the introduction of cellulose paint in 1925, for this was tougher than the old type paint and did not scratch so easily. It could be washed and polished in a few minutes, and in addition it made repairs to damaged bodywork both faster and more satisfactory, as it was much easier to match colours. Two years later in 1927 an even greater benefit for the car owner who looked after his own car was the adoption of chromium instead of the age-old nickel plate. True the first chromium plate tended to grow 'ulcers' if neglected but this was soon overcome.

Then buffers, which had appeared first back in 1908 in isolated instances, became more popular. At first they were unsightly, heavy, expensive and complicated with steel springs supporting large steel or rubber pads fore and aft, or spring-backed buffers similar to those used for locomotives on the railway. But, very gradually they too became sensible. Mind you the original designs were on the whole very efficient. One car could collide with another yet the buffers would reduce damage to a minimum which cannot be said of cars today.

But it was William Morris who made the next great advance when in 1927 he gambled on the future success of the body made by gigantic presses and in great quantities. Morris had studied this problem when he visited the United States and knew what was required to make a body at extremely low cost. But all depended on the demand which in turn depended on the population. America had a huge home market. No European country was in the same happy position.

Fortune was favourable – though the cost of the first bodies from the Morris plant must have been astronomic – and Morris cars soon showed that their creator's ideas were right. After that it was essential for all manufacturers who wished to keep up with the times to adopt the same idea unless their success depended on selling a few marvellously built vehicles to those who could afford them.

Mass-production had then, as it has now to a lesser extent, its difficulties. If very expensive machinery is used it is essential to have a long run of the same work to make a profit, hence the difficulty in making any sudden change due to fashion or the abrupt appearance of a rival car.

At last all energies were directed towards providing cars for family use, cars designed to be run by their owners with the minimum of trouble and expenditure of time. The days when more and more power to provide more and more speed but with no particular effort

This racing model Packard is driven here by Ralph DePalma in 1919. He was one of the greatest pioneer racing-drivers of that time.

to serve 'ordinary' people had gone. Professional drivers, 'chauffeurs', were in less demand since the type of person now using cars was unable to afford them. Repair garages were becoming service stations, though on no highly organized plan as yet. Petrol and oil were easily obtainable, though more expensive than before, and the laws of motoring were rapidly increasing in number in every motoring country in the world.

Much was happening too among the famous firms of the industry. The British Daimler Company was now building large, comfortable, five-seater cars with good performance, and well up to the standard of their earlier reputation. The Knight engine had faded out and an amalgamation with the British Small Arms concern had assisted financially.

Rolls-Royce were going from strength to strength, again with the large luxurious car beautifully made and with every desirable fitting known to man. Cadillac were coming to the fore in America with a reputation

for special cars built to millionaires' specifications. Mercedes too, were gradually recovering their market after the war, though they had never lost their world-wide reputation. There was no question however of mass-production for this type of car.

But there were also newcomers who were intruding with vigour and success. For sheer style, style suggesting power in abundance allied with spectacular attraction, the new Hispano-Suizas could not be beaten and were even difficult to equal. Many explanations of this car's curious name have been given, for it means Spanish-Swiss, but none of them seems convincing, since the car was always accepted as French. Ownership of an Hispano was a definite mark of social position in the motoring world, and the firm also built a number of very special, big, closed cars for the rich. These big machines gave the industry great prestige all over the world in a way nothing else could have done, for they provided travel in the most comfortable possible circumstances.

In direct contrast were the new French Citroëns, cars sponsored by that possessor of boundless energy, André Citroën, whose name had first appeared in connection with a bevel gear with unusual teeth, and which ran more silently than the standard pattern gear could ever achieve. Two of these V-shaped teeth form the badge of the car today.

Citroën had managed to bring out a new small car in 1919, a small car built in great numbers and which was excellent value for money. But the reason why this created a definite sensation was that for the first time in Europe an assembly line was used on the American pattern. By 1921 Citroëns were leaving the factory at the rate of 10,000 a year, in 1926 a factory was taken over in England by them and by 1929 annual output was 100,000 vehicles. André was driven by the same idea that had urged William Morris on, namely the provision of the sort of car which the majority of people could afford to purchase, and also afford to run.

The so-called five h.p. two-seater was to be seen by the hundred in France by 1923, and 1934 saw a large, almost revolutionary design with a most useful four-seater saloon body, a new type of suspension giving a smooth and comfortable ride and, of all things, front-wheel drive. The effect of all this on the older quietly efficient firms was revolutionary.

By 1930 there were plenty of cars for the family from which to choose, for instance, the new Austin 12, which was a scaled down version of the earlier 20 h.p., the Morris, the larger Singers and Hillmans, the Peugeots, Renaults, and the pleasant little Fiat 501.

Top: A Chrysler of 1926. The normal saloon car of this period was not startlingly original, nor were the different makes easily distinguishable. But the body was both commodious and comfortable, and this was particularly noticeable with American cars, for at last they were starting to give as much thought to the body as the chassis.

Bottom: The six-cylinder Napier. The appearance of this car prompted other British manufacturers to think hard about six-cylinder units, when they were only making four-cylinder cars. Due to the persuasive drive of Selwyn Edge of Napiers, the Napier soon came to the forefront of the range of luxury cars.

Top: The Ford Model T had given way to the Model A in 1927. Mass-production had made Ford's prices incredibly low: in 1909 the Model T's price was $850, in 1912 it was $600, in 1918 $450 and in 1926 it cost $380. This is a Model A of 1928, and it was also excellent value for money.

Bottom: The Peugeot Coupé d'affaire 201 of 1929. This model proved very popular and was produced in quantity for some years. It is interesting that these cars had engines which were then considered very small, but which are now regarded as quite powerful—big enough to carry a full two- or even four-seater body with no trouble.

To add to the interest of the period much was happening on the engineering side. First of all tyres of greatly increased section known as 'balloons' were introduced. Run at much lower pressure than those of the older type the new tyres gave a more comfortable ride, but the steering design had not been ready for the change. One car I owned was fitted with these tyres and all went well until it reached 60 m.p.h. At that speed suddenly an appalling 'shimmy' developed, steering control vanished abruptly and the machine bounced off both verges of the road.

Then suspension came in for an overhaul, it was considered that the old, familiar, half-elliptic springs were no longer the best form to use. Soon car after car appeared with independent suspension for each front wheel, while some had independent suspension for all four

wheels. Again teething troubles introduced rather horrific eccentricities. For example one car which I drove put a hind wheel up after a bump, but did not put it down again, and it was quite a shock.

Bodies were developing as well. There soon became a demand for a body which could be closed comfortably in bad weather but could be open when the sun shone; an attempt to have the best of everything for the cost of one. The result was the 'Allweather' body which amounted to a more substantial hood, easily erected and secured, plus side windows, or firm side screens very different from the original flapping 'curtains'. At first prone to trouble because wear caused air leaks and distortion this design gradually improved, although, after the first spate of popularity it lost favour, save in America where the weather was more reliable. This innovation was accompanied by a body with a 'sunshine' roof; a small section of the roof above the front seats could be slid back in fair weather. But the 1935 designs were liable to leak under heavy rain or to jam in the guides if used rarely, and a good deal of experiment was necessary before these defects were overcome.

Another type of body had much more success. Away back in the days of the horse, owners of country estates often possessed a special carriage built to transport either luggage in quantity or visitors from the nearest railway station, a kind of all-purpose vehicle. This could be used also for taking guns out on the estate when a shoot was organized. Hence the name 'Station Wagon' 'Shooting Brake' or 'Estate Car' according to personal taste. Back in 1903 Panhards had built a 'Station Omnibus' for the same purpose. Now some manufacturers, Daimler and Austin, for example, catalogued a car of this type to see what demand there might be. They were not what one could term beautiful vehicles, the body was as long as the chassis could take and constructed with upright and horizontal wood girders to which flat steel panels could be attached. This was an inexpensive form of construction – the vehicle could carry people or a bulky, very large load, which was the chief consideration, and appearance came second.

Year by year accessories on the market multiplied. In 1933 most cars had some form of turn indicator usually of unduly elaborate form. There were metal hands which could be extended to one side or the other as required, illuminated fingers similarly arranged, white arrows in a panel which could be illuminated to indicate which way a car was to turn, and that same year Morris cars appeared with a miniature traffic light signal of green, amber, and red lights to show the driver's intention. The latter stirred the authorities immediately since real traffic lights were then being used, especially in France, and the contraption had to be removed.

Screen wipers developed also, the original clumsy hand-operated affairs being superseded by electrically actuated arms, more fragile than, but similar to, those which were to become universal for many years.

All the cars of this period were high by modern standards but this was not such a defect as people might think. A car of this period was much easier to get into or out of than the car of today, while the relatively upright seats gave more space for the passengers' feet, and therefore more comfort.

Cars were now being used for holiday runs over long distances and even taken abroad for weeks at a time. Consequently accommodation for the occupants' luggage had to be taken into account. At first this consisted of a steel slat or bar carrier sold as an extra and mounted over the petrol tank at the rear of the car, and if the carrier was loaded, it often made refilling awkward. Then special 'trunks' were made to go on the carrier. Very gradually, around 1925, bodies were extended to form a tail compartment with a door and lid, the best of which were on American cars, and the worst on the French and German machines. But at all events they were the ancestors of the large 'boots' we have today.

It is doubtful whether there will ever be again a period in which development was so definite and speedy as from 1918 to 1938. Obviously components which prove successful and are attractive will be adopted by every firm in turn in various forms: therefore the design of cars tends to level out. But as time goes by there are fewer and fewer new things to consider, since the standard reached is already satisfactory and any change entails a great deal of expense.

From 1922 onwards cars had to have brakes on all four wheels or fall from favour. Initial efforts to provide this had exciting results. No two manufacturers agreed on the form of operation, which could vary from a collection of rods and pressure-equalizing devices to simple cables which all too often failed to apply all the brakes with equal pressure. Then there was fierce argument as to whether it was best to control the front brakes with the pedal, the rear ones with the hand lever, or vice versa, or have all four brakes applied by the pedal alone. If the last, there arose the question of how to arrange for the separate 'emergency' brake required by law. It was all onc big worry and the experiments which took place greatly increased the cost of manufacture.

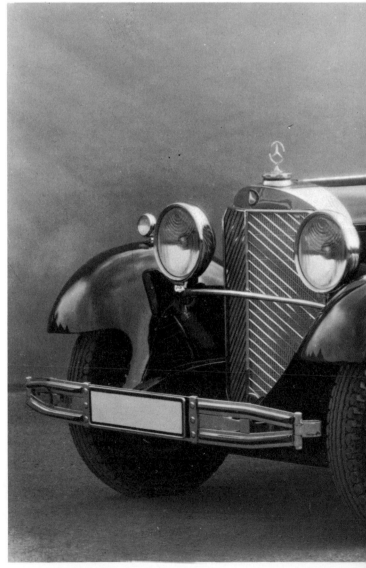

Top right: The Aston-Martin was a fast car with a fine reputation. It was the custom then not only to bring the exhaust pipes out at the side of the bonnet, but also to ornament them and the silencer with metal. Note that the screen is arranged to lie flat on this 1934/36 model, as on all sports cars at that time.

Bottom: The big, open, four-seater Mercedes of 1930. It was easily recognized as such, because the radiator grille resembles the original striking Mercedes radiator. The styling of the car conceals the high speed of which this Mercedes was capable.

But by 1927 four-wheel brakes were an established component and no longer the subject of frightful rumours originating from unfortunate experience. But as the period came to a close and the fateful year 1939 loomed near it was obvious that one very important change in components passed without due recognition for what it was – the greatest aid for a driver yet conceived. Over in the States experiments had proved that a fully automatic gear change was possible, thus removing the last real control difficulty drivers faced. The experiments came to fruition in 1939 when the G.M. (General Motors) Hydramatic appeared first on the Oldsmobile car, next on the Cadillac, but, curiously enough, did not create a great deal of interest among the public.

As early as 1928 Armstrong-Siddeley had adopted an unusual gearbox, designed by a man called Wilson, with which the driver only had to move a small lever to a notch on a plain quadrant then depress and release the clutch pedal for the gear to change automatically. No skill was required, and no effort. Then in 1931 Daimler used a redesigned version of a German device as a clutch and called it the Fluid Flywheel. Since Daimler now had the Lanchester experience of planetary gears to draw upon and these were similar to the Wilson gearbox, the combination of the Fluid Flywheel and a planetary gearbox was an obvious improvement.

The 'Fluid Flywheel' was similar to a turbine which drove only when the engine speed had risen to a certain figure and then did so very smoothly. Applied to the Wilson gear the effect was to make control much easier since the driver only had to open the throttle to engage a gear and did not have a clutch pedal at all. Obviously this made driving quite simple as far as control was concerned, and it seems curious that the idea

was not an immediate and revolutionary success everywhere. However the seed which was to grow into full automation was already there, both for Armstrong-Siddeley and Daimler.

Another novelty which appeared did not have the same promise. For racing engines a supercharger had been adopted widely, the reason being that by pumping gas into the cylinder more power could be obtained than in the ordinary way by sucking it in. A number of attempts to supercharge production engines occurred, with unhappy results. But Mercedes did produce a fantastic car in 1937 with a supercharged 5½-litre, eight-cylinder engine which was reasonably successful. The supercharger only came into operation if the throttle pedal was fully depressed, which was safer; and it may be interesting to note that the engine developed 115 h.p. until the supercharger started, and then went up to 180 h.p. But this was not for normal motoring.

As fitting finale to a wonderful period, yet another car especially intended to provide the world with inexpensive, reliable transport was produced in Germany. Apparently sponsored by Adolf Hitler, if one could judge from the propaganda, this car, the Volkswagen, i.e. The People's Car, was a reasonably-sized four-seater, with an air-cooled, four-cylinder engine in the tail. Although slightly crude maybe and not particularly quiet, the idea behind it was excellent, as has been proved through the years.

But 1938 was once again a period of growing international tension, apprehension over Hitler was increasing, and the new machine was not accorded the interest it deserved by other countries' designers, indeed it was the subject for rather misplaced humour. In Britain we were on the eve of another war, and the manufacture of cars for civilians no longer counted.

It was due to the Bentleys that the British held on to some vestige of their reputation against the onslaught of the competition from the Continent. At Le Mans, during the Twenties, the line of Bentleys consistently doing well, held everyone's attention. In fact the Bentleys won at Le Mans four times running, as no car did before, and none has since. This is a Bentley of 1922. They were produced for six years, and were just the cars which the wealthy young Englishman had been waiting for. They were ferocious machines, but yet were docile enough to drive to a tea-dance in Mayfair.

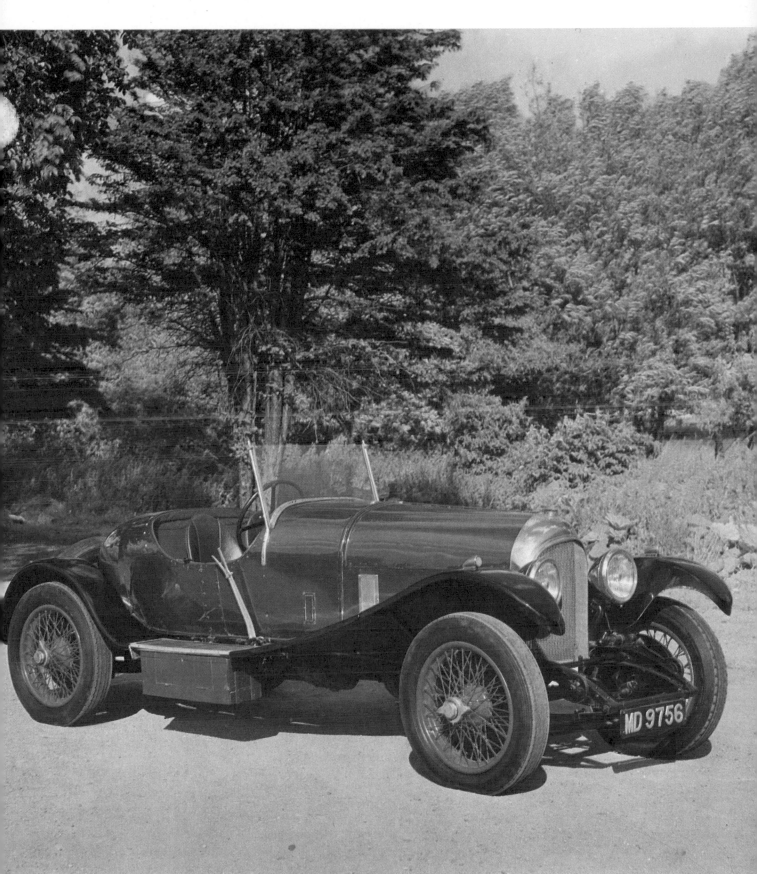

THE GREAT MERGERS

Preceding pages: The modern Vauxhall plant at Luton. In 1951 the Morris and Austin companies, comprising 33 concerns in all, merged to become the British Motor Corporation. Each works still retained their individuality, but could now take advantage of the others' special facilities. *Below*: One of the far-reaching results of this great merger was the Mini, which first appeared in 1959. With the revolutionary transverse engine and by using the parts with separate modifications, a number of different models, each based on the same fundamental design, could now be produced. *Below right*: The vast change which has taken place in car production over the years has resulted in this sort of plant layout. This picture shows the Austin Longbridge assembly-line of Austin 1100s. *Right*: The men who pioneered the vast change were William Morris, afterwards Lord Nuffield (left), and Herbert Austin, afterwards Lord Austin of Longbridge (right). *Left*: The British Motor Corporation symbol.

Below: The Ford Production-line of 1913. This frame, called the 'body drop', is just that. The body slides down a ramp, and, with the help of chains, lands on the chassis, which has been wheeled into position.
Right: In the car plants of today, however, the car moves to its skilled workman, whereas in the early days the craftsmen moved to the cars. This series of huge conveyor systems make up part of the enormous, sprawling Fiat works in Turin. The car today no longer has a separate chassis, because the body-unit is now made of stressed steel, with the engine and transmission mounted on a light sub-frame.

Once again the world had changed. Because of the war money was more evenly distributed though it was harder to earn and its value was less. The men who worked in factories no longer came to the works on bicycles as they had done in thousands when the motor industry was young, they all wanted cars and wanted them at once.

Everyone was a potential motorist, and more important still, women at last drove on equal terms with men. At last the car could become transport for the family. As long as only the male handled the wheel the car had to remain his private possession. But now feminine interest had to be borne in mind whenever a new model was designed – its styling, colouring and accessories took on a new importance. Although money was scarce, and very few people could afford it, the pervading idea seemed to be that a family could not exist without a car. People went to work in cars, unless it was faster to get there by train, in which case people drove to the station. The children were driven to school, fetched from it, people shopped by car, visited friends by car. Perishable goods, raw materials and awkward loads began to be transported in heavy lorries by road.

But as far as the car manufacturing works were concerned it was none too easy to convert them from war to peace work, from making weapons to cars. The whole layout of the factory was wrong, almost every item had to be altered for greater productivity and yet during all this hurly burly new designs had to be evolved which included all the latest innovations. To make matters more complicated, somehow the older models had still to be produced incorporating a few modifications, as speedily as possible, to meet the immense demand.

But the most urgent problem was how to modernize and convert the factories, which the frenzied production of war weapons had now proved to be unwieldy. How much work this entailed may be judged by the rapid alterations to Austin's Longbridge plant. Machines with their shafting had to be removed and the latest electrically-powered machines installed in a quite different pattern. Assembly lines had to be planned and installed, each with rows of bins containing the necessary parts so that assemblers need move the shortest possible distance to obtain what was wanted. All through the factory it

became cheaper to use machines instead of skilled men. At the end of each engine assembly-line a testing rig replaced the old testhouse with its special horse-power testing brakes. Every second of work had to be accounted for. In 1910 over a hundred men worked to produce a car in a week, in 1926 the number was sixteen, and under the new scheme the millionth Austin was made by just nine men.

All this reorganization was the forerunner of vast underground conveyors, automated body-building sections, which contributed to the tremendous increase in production. But for the moment all manufacturers had to exist on new versions of their pre-war models, though some American factories were lucky enough to have continued car manufacture throughout the war.

The designers were busy too, since a real family car at low cost was urgently needed. Moreover, the days of the chassis designer as a power to be obeyed implicitly were numbered. Gradually the body design began to govern the layout of mechanism. Since low cost depended on quantity fewer firms producing greater numbers of the same model achieved the best profits.

So the larger firms set about gobbling up their smaller contemporaries. The huge organization which Morris, now Lord Nuffield, had created, absorbed Riley, M.G., Wolseley, a carburetter firm called S.U., a number of accessory concerns, and spread works all over the British countryside.

Before the war all of us had been intrigued by Sunbeam making an agreement with Talbot, whose cars bore the crest of the Earl of Shrewsbury and Talbot for a badge, and the old time French firm of Darracq. This led to a difficulty which was becoming more and more prevalent, that of recognizing which car was which. This combine was taken over by Rootes just after the war to form another huge concern including Humber, Singer and Hillman. Rolls-Royce, surprisingly, absorbed Bentleys. And to complete the picture Standard and Triumph combined; Aston-Martin took over Lagonda; Rovers controlled the new Alvis. Mind you the older school of man who retained a personal affection for the individual makes of cars found these changes difficult to appreciate, and famous firms in history appeared likely to lose their identity.

Preceding pages: Some of the results of modern car production, and the problems which have arisen from it are here seen in a picture of the car park at Wembley Stadium, London, on Cup Final day.
Below: The evolution in styling in American and British cars is apparent from these 'family trees' of the

models produced by the three car groups—Chrysler, British Ford and General Motors.
Left: The Dodge car through the years from 1915 to 1955.
Right: The British Ford from 1923 to 1949. Production of Ford cars was started in Britain in 1911 in Manchester, and not until 1931 did the works move to Dagenham. The

All this did not in fact take place immediately after the war, but the facts are grouped because this was the biggest change ever to affect motoring as a whole. The change was not confined to Britain. In France those motoring pioneers who were still alive received a shock when Citroën, that very vigorous newcomer to the world of car manufacturers, took over the greatest firm in France's motoring history – Panhards. In the United States since 1918 General Motors had controlled Buick, Cadillac, Pontiac, Oldsmobile, Chevrolet, La Salle, Welch, Randolph, Scripps-Booth, Sheridan, Viking, and Marquette, and took over the Australian Holden in 1948 to constitute another immense empire. But American influence went further still. American money from 1926 sustained Vauxhalls; the Rootes group is now owned by the huge Chrysler Corporation; Ford had become an enormous power in the world with works in many countries.

But the real sensation occurred in 1951 when Morris and Austin merged as one huge concern named the British Motor Corporation, with each enormous works retaining its individuality, though taking advantage of the others' special facilities. In this combine were included a big bodyworks, various accessory firms, and overseas plants – 33 concerns in all, merging their interests and welded into one body.

All through the history of the car industry it has been the men of character who have made all the difference to the cars we use today, and not necessarily the chief designers. Herbert Austin and William Richard Morris were two excellent examples of this.

Herbert Austin was born in 1866. His father was a farmer, his mother the daughter of a naval captain. At 16, he became an apprentice to his uncle who controlled a general engineering works in Melbourne, Australia, and then worked for many other engineering firms gaining invaluable basic experience in his chosen craft. At 18 Austin had acquired engineering knowledge beyond his years, together with a practical knowledge of craftsmen's standards. So it is not surprising that at 27 he was asked by Frederick Wolseley to return and take a hand in the Wolseley Tool and Sheepshearing Company's activities in Birmingham. Nor is it surprising that he became extremely interested in the news about 'horseless carriages' which was filtering through from Germany and France in 1894-5, or that, working in his spare time, he actually produced a car of his own design in 1895. This car had tiller-steering and three wheels but it was to be the ancestor of the cars the huge B.M.C. combine now produces.

first two cars illustrated here are Model Ts, the third a Model F, the fourth the CX 10 HP, and the fifth is the Anglia.

Far right: General Motors milestone cars. First, the 1908 Cadillac was built the year that General Motors was founded. Second is a 1919 Oldsmobile, which was the one millionth car produced. Third is a Buick of 1929 which was General Motors' 10 millionth car. Fourth, in 1940 Chevrolet produced General Motors' 25 millionth car, and fifth, in 1954 the 50 millionth General Motors' car rolled off a Chevrolet assembly-line.

Car production had not ceased during the war in America, and therefore styling, etc., had improved and was still improving, while Europe was still frantically trying to revert to peace-time work. The gulf which existed after the Second World War is exemplified in these pictures.

Top: The first post-war Hillman Minx which appeared in 1945, and although a revised version of a pre-war model it had no less than 57 improvements in detail.
Bottom: The 1949 Buick, which has a distinct essence of modern styling about it.

Knighted in 1917 for the work his factories did during the First World War he became Lord Austin of Longbridge in 1936, neither honour changing his character by the smallest fraction, or his determination to attain the target he had in mind. The title he took of Lord Longbridge goes back to his discovery of a derelict metal box factory while cycling round Longbridge in 1905, which grew to the immense Austin Longbridge factory which exists today.

William Morris grew up with the same intense desire to make motoring more than just a pleasure for the few, to provide cars for the millions, and from the commencement of his career he steadfastly adhered to this ideal. He, however, fostered his interest in transport very differently from Austin. William Richard Morris was born in 1877 in Worcester, and was brought to Oxford at the age of three by his parents, Frederick and Ann. His first job was in a cycle shop, after which he himself set up business mending cycles in his parent's back-yard shed in James Street, Oxford. That was in 1892 and it is alleged that his capital was £4.

The shop prospered, Morris making cycles and racing them with success. His interest soon centred on cars, although this brought him near to financial disaster more often than was pleasant. But in a very short time he bought a disused schoolroom in Cowley for a work-

Top: A smaller model Rolls-Royce. Although it maintained the dignity inseparable from all Rolls designs, the size of the car naturally lost some of its impression of luxury, comfortable as it was. In fact, the smaller car never seemed to suit the Derby firm.

Bottom: A Pontiac of 1952. This car in fact was one of 11 Pontiac models which were introduced that year, and is an indication of the high production level America had achieved when the rest of the world was still recovering from the war.

shop in which to assemble a car of his own, and, though no one realized it at the time, that constituted the founding of his empire. This was also the beginning of Morris Garages, which was always to remain his particular pride and joy, even when the factory moved to Abingdon. It was Cecil Kimber, his manager, who commenced drawing new chassis from the main Cowley works in order to convert them into sports cars, an idea which succeeded so well that in 1929 larger premises were essential. These Kimber found to form the basis of the present M.G. factory in a building which had been built by the Pavlova Leather Company in Abingdon during the First World War and then abandoned.

To return to William Morris. Throughout his life his sole ambition was bent on providing a family car for the populace, a car at a low price and completely equipped with all those accessories which were extras for most cars. Moreover, he was determined the car should be built more efficiently than any of those he had seen during a visit to the United States in 1925. Here he spent much time studying American methods of production, and the result of this was the creation of the Pressed Steel Company in 1926 at Cowley near Oxford to make steel bodies on American lines. This works was to influence future cars, quite apart from Morris.

Morris was always a very difficult, autocratic, little

Top: A sports car of 1940—the C type Aston Martin. The first Aston Martin appeared in 1921, and it is a tribute to the firm's unflagging zeal and the excellence of the engine, though the company has changed hands several times through the years, that the car is still considered one of the most beautiful thoroughbreds.

Bottom: The Sunbeam Mark III Saloon. Now overdrive could be an optional extra, being standard on the Alpine model. Though the radiator grille suggests that the car comes from the old Sunbeam stable, fashion has changed everything else. Polished hub caps have now been provided to cover the spokes and hub.

There is now a marked change to be seen in the design of cars, as these pictures show.
Top: The front-drive seven h.p. Citroën of 1934.
Centre above: A Peugeot made up until 1949. Note that the headlamps are situated under the radiator grille close together, and it has a sunshine roof.

Centre below: The four h.p. Renault 'Sport'. The form of the car has changed radically from its predecessors, in order to give it a new look.
Bottom: A Ford Prefect of 1949. Attention has been concentrated on making the body larger and more comfortable, whilst maintaining a relatively low price.

man, but he achieved what he had set out to do with no small success. It was he who insisted that his austere, open two-seater put on the market in 1931 must positively cost no more than £100, which was no mean feat at that time. For his incredible generosity to hospitals, universities, charities, etc., he was made a Baron – Lord Nuffield – in 1934, and was raised to a Viscount in 1938. It is said that Morris bought the Nuffield estate simply because he had some slight difficulty in joining the local golf club, which done, he found he also owned a pub, a fact not without humour as Nuffield had strong views about alcoholic refreshment.

Contemporaries of his alleged, and I can well believe it, that when he had achieved his immense car empire and title he would have liked to have another small cycle shop to run as a relief from the incessant problems and political conundrums inevitable when mass-production becomes a national asset as well as big business.

But as far as the rest of the industry was concerned, there were still quite a few problems to iron out. At the works, planning for the new cars was complicated by the fact that design had radically changed since before the war, and it was very difficult to assess how much this fact would influence buyers. A drastic change in fashion can be a world-record flop or a magnificent success, but few inspired prophets could ever guess which it would be in advance.

As a whole, motorists were accustomed to the radiator being level with, or just behind the front axle. Now the latest cars from the United States had the shell representing the radiator some way in front of the axle while the stern end 'boot' extended much more to the rear than had been normal practice. Consequently the car grew much longer, and many thought the result horrible. On the other hand there was no denying that concentrating all the seats well towards the centre of the car had advantages, since it made for a more comfortable ride, and the obvious step was to increase the wheel-base to attain this end.

It was not only the car manufacturers who were faced with a mass of urgent problems difficult to solve. Every supplier of essential materials was in the same boat, every factory in the land needed drastic alteration to fit it out for peace work. Often very irritating delays in the vital supply of that material occurred without which production of cars could not proceed to schedule. Add to this the fact that, as living costs had soared, everyone demanded more pay and wanted it at once, and it can be seen that the production of cars in Europe was anything but an easy job after the Second World War.

CARS THE WORLD WANTED

BUT MAY SOON FORGET?

Many manufacturers now market estate cars. These are always extremely popular with big families, or for use in the country. Their great advantage is that they provide more room for luggage of any kind. *Top left* is the Mini, with wood strips curiously reminis-cent of the horse-carriage. *Top right* is the Renault 4 with a counter-balanced rear door. *Bottom left* is the Peugeot 404 estate car. *Bottom right* is the Hillman Super Minx. In each case the accommodation for four or more occupants remains unchanged.

Up to 1948 most cars were still revised versions of the pre-war models. Plans for new models were very much influenced by the general financial situation in Europe. On paper, everyone appeared to be wealthier, yet every country was faced with rising costs. Taxes were spiralling upwards and motoring was bearing an increasing part of these, directly and indirectly. In every country of Europe petrol prices had risen astronomically, and in countries such as France and Italy the cost of petrol rose so high that the foreign motorist intending to tour abandoned the idea.

Therefore the provision of cars which would be economical to run was more urgent than ever before. The European motor industry responded vigorously to the challenge and the new cars were exactly what was wanted, for they were not only economical to run but cost less than had been expected; and furthermore their performance was far better than even the optimists had hoped for. And so at long last the real family car had become a reality.

The first sensation was the appearance of the Morris Minor in an entirely new form, a car of just the right type, comfortable, economical and handy. This new Morris had a side-valve engine of 918 c.c. in a two-door saloon which definitely had style. Appearing first in 1948 it has gone through many transformations and is popular even to this day. In October, 1948 an open version was added, and in September, 1950 a four-door saloon. But the two-door saloon remained the favourite, because it was less expensive and safer. In July, 1952 there came another version with the same lines but an overhead-valve engine of 803 c.c., which produced the same power, and in 1962 came the 948 c.c. engined car, then the 1098 c.c. of today in a two- or four-door saloon, an open-bodied version, or a Traveller model.

The estate car became gradually more and more popular even for much larger cars than the Morris Minor, with the result that one of the American versions of today, the 'Prairie Waggon' Ford is nearly twenty feet long overall.

William Morris' dream of cars for the million came true with these Morris cars.
Top left is one of the later versions of the Morris Minor, this model being an estate car.
Bottom left is the normal Morris Minor 1000 four-seater saloon.

Right is one of the original Morris Minors, which had a side valve engine of 848 c.c. This car appeared first in 1948, and still sells successfully today with an engine of 1098 c.c.

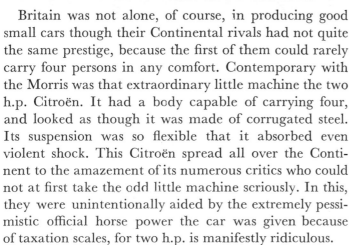

Britain was not alone, of course, in producing good small cars though their Continental rivals had not quite the same prestige, because the first of them could rarely carry four persons in any comfort. Contemporary with the Morris was that extraordinary little machine the two h.p. Citroën. It had a body capable of carrying four, and looked as though it was made of corrugated steel. Its suspension was so flexible that it absorbed even violent shock. This Citroën spread all over the Continent to the amazement of its numerous critics who could not at first take the odd little machine seriously. In this, they were unintentionally aided by the extremely pessimistic official horse power the car was given because of taxation scales, for two h.p. is manifestly ridiculous.

Nevertheless with characteristic Citroën verve the car attained marked success, because of its cheapness and easy maintenance. Annual output of Citroëns had numbered 24,445 vehicles by 1947, and the effect of the small car was to raise this to 200,000 by 1957. In Italy, too, Fiats had produced a wide range of small, economi-

cal cars which were to become very popular indeed, and which were to provide scores upon scores of people with just the form of transport they required. These little machines were legitimate successors to the little Fiat of 1936, which was always referred to as the 'Mouse' and which had been succeeded by a similar 500 c.c. car named the Balilla. But the models with which the great Turin firm flooded the Continent from now onwards were the two-cylinder, air-cooled 500, the four-cylinder, water-cooled 600 and the 850, also water-cooled. All these cars had the engine tucked away at the rear, all had independent suspension for the four wheels, and their speed ranged from 65 to 80 m.p.h., their fuel consumption a gallon for some 40 to 60 miles. An astonishing performance for the type of car. The 500 was available as a station wagon, the 600 was available with a Multipla body – a very small coach-like affair with ample room for plenty of luggage – while the 850 could be a saloon or a coupé, in which case it could attain 84 m.p.h. and cover 34 miles on a gallon of fuel. It

was small wonder that any stream of vehicles in Italy was mostly composed of small Fiats; or that the Fiat works has now grown to an immense size, the car factory alone occupying 520 acres, containing 100 miles of conveyor line, and even 14 miles of railway track.

Meantime Renault were flooding France with their little rear-engined 750s, another car suitable for ordinary family use.

It had been obvious from the very first years after the war that engineers were not being bound by conventional ideas of car design. But though the type of cars Citroën, Renault and Fiat had produced were a decided shock to most motorists of experience, and even more so to motoring enthusiasts, it was nothing compared to the shock they received from B.M.C. in 1959.

The immense British concern suddenly announced an Austin Seven and a Morris Mini. One look at these new cars made it plain that the really reliable family car had arrived at last, a car able to carry four with their luggage, a car which looked just right, a car with plenty of power from its four-cylinder, 848 c.c. engine, and very economical into the bargain. Here for the first time was a design – by Alex Issigonis – which could be a Morris in one form and an Austin in another. The word Mini was a winner from the start and the Austin had to be renamed Mini almost immediately, as people called them all Minis anyway. The main cause for the shock, however, was that the car was a body in which the machinery had been mounted afterwards, though very neatly – a public demonstration that our old ideas had gone by the board, that the body was the principal thing, the engine and its auxiliaries now just secondary. The engine was placed compactly under a very short bonnet in front, together with the gearbox and final drive to the front wheels, as neat an arrangement as anyone could desire. This was a new departure, for front-wheel drive had been regarded as unsatisfactory for years, despite the fact that Citroëns had introduced it in 1934 and used this transmission for their successful 1938 six-cylinder car.

It now became obvious that the new cars were more B.M.C. than individual, in other words the combine could make a basic car in vast numbers then incorporate certain variations under different 'makes'. A Wolseley Mini called a Hornet followed with a 998 c.c. engine, then the Riley Elf, each had differences apart from their special radiator shells which resembled the original radiator designs. The Wolseley, for example, had a quite different boot. To add to the excitement a fast version appeared called the Mini-Cooper.

Some recent trends in styling.
Top: The 1966 Buick Riviera from General Motors. It is interesting to note the ornamental, but quite useless, imitation racing hub nuts.

Centre left: The Volvo 132S, designed and built in Sweden.
Centre right: The incredibly popular Ford Prefect was remarkable value for its price.
Bottom: The Honda Sports car.

You have only to watch traffic at the weekend in any European country to see that the Minis have succeeded beyond their designers' wildest dreams, and accessories specially produced for Minis have flourished. Of the various types of Mini the Traveller is almost the ideal family car, especially with the all-steel body. Adults have a good deal of leg room, children can be safe in the rear seat, but behind that seat is a large compartment extending right to the end of the car which stores mountains of luggage more easily than in a boot. It is even possible to carry more luggage on a roof rack. The cost of the normal Mini as I write is £413 in 1967; (all prices are subject to a variable tax increase). It is true to say that Minis changed the whole idea of motoring, thousands of families could now have a car which they could never have afforded before.

There followed in the Minis' wake the larger Vauxhall Viva, the Hillman Imp with the engine at the rear, and both cost £445 in deluxe form. B.M.C. then added the larger 1100 c.c. at around £500, to their range. Here again the car took many names, Austin, Morris, Wolseley, M.G., Riley, each with variations but all family cars. The Ford factories in Britain, which had also grown to huge size, had got into their stride as soon as any other manufacturer. But there had been a big change.

Away back in 1931 Henry Ford had decided that the Model T was at the end of its useful life, though there were many who did not agree with him. The change over to a new model entailed an enormous amount of reorganization. Delays to the plan drove Henry to a fine frenzy at times with consequent criticism of his subordinates, who in turn were driven to cold fury. But the upshot was a new car and one having no resemblance to the Model T, a quite normal type of car in fact.

The new factory at Dagenham took to pouring out 115,000 vehicles in 1947, among them Anglias and Prefects, the Anglia body from an older model being supplied as a Popular at £275. All these cars were definitely family vehicles at low cost, and people with a little more money were offered the larger Zephyrs and Consuls in 1948, which incorporated the first fully post-war design of a V8 3½-litre engine.

Yet another shock for the critics came from France and very much upset veteran motorists into the bargain. The most famous firm in motoring, the concern which had made France the premier country in car manufacture, and which had won so many great races in earlier heroic days, Panhard-Levassor, in 1946 came out with a most extraordinary small car powered by an air-cooled horizontal engine with two opposed cylinders. A car no one would ever think might come from Panhard's in any circumstances, and it was yet another symbol that austerity and economy ruled.

The luxurious vehicles had not disappeared as one might have thought. Rolls-Royce now provided a V eight-cylinder car of 6230 c.c. and some 12 feet in length, just as carefully made and supervised as ever before. True, their clients had changed from royalty to dictators and presidents, while top executives in big firms now used the cars as symbols of prestige. Daimlers had built large, magnificent-looking cars for our royalty after the war, cars with 12-cylinder V engines and with what appeared to be miles of bonnet. The 4.5-litre Majestic in 1960 was an attempt to return to a smaller car which could have a specialist body on request, the last of the big cars having been built in 1953. These cars had coachwork designed for maximum comfort and luxury.

Over in Germany Mercedes-Benz had recovered from the chaos created by the war and their products were still the prestige cars on the Continent. Their long range of different cars soon became bewildering. There was no suggestion of American influence here, but it is interesting that the huge firm of Mercedes-Benz is now obviously considering closer relations between all the German car firms beneficial. This idea resulted in the establishment of the Deutsche Automobilgesellschaft in 1966, a combination between Mercedes-Benz and Volkswagen for their mutual assistance, in which both companies have an equal financial interest, equal rights and equal obligations. Technical and financial resources of both companies will be pooled. Once more the value of creating one huge concern is made obvious.

Without doubt, the luxury car of the Mercedes series, the car which really had universal prestige, was the enormous '600', powered by a 6300 c.c. V8 engine, giving some 250 h.p. For this car everything possible was automatic, all the windows could be raised or lowered by pressing buttons, the suspension, which was pneumatic, could be adjusted by the driver to suit the circumstance. The front and rear seats were electrically adjustable, also the boot lid and all door locks were electrically operated. This was the most modern of the European luxury cars and incidentally the most expensive – a 600 cost almost £10,000 to a British buyer.

Volkswagen itself had come into its own and was no longer a subject for humour, but acknowledged as a worthy family car and nicknamed officially the 'Beetle'

Impudence versus dignity.

Top left: The later version of the 'deux chevaux', the two h.p. Citroën, an incredibly popular and ubiquitous car.

Top right: The Renault Dauphine, one of the world's most thoroughly proved cars.

Centre: The long and stately Chevrolet Caprice.

Bottom: Another American luxury car, the Cadillac Fleetwood Brougham. Inside it sports carpeted foot rests, adjustable swivel-type reading lamps, and two illuminated fold-down utility trays.

Popular-priced cars, and all value for money.

Top: The Mini De Luxe. All Minis are now made with Hydrolastic suspension.

Centre left: Small though the Mini is, it is very sturdy, and can carry a roof rack, or even a boat, as seen here.

Centre right: The Triumph Herald, a design which has been most successful, and produced for some years now. Its popular characteristic is its very small turning circle. This Herald has had a sunshine roof fitted, which can now be fitted to most cars.

Bottom left: The Riley Elf, another version of the Mini. but it retains its familiar Riley radiator shell.

Bottom right: The Italian 500 c.c. Fiat which is very popular not only in Italy but elsewhere in Europe.
Below: Modern design has many facets, as this Citroën Ami 6 shows. It has a pleasant design, which belies its essential utility.

in Germany. By 1950, 81,979 Volkswagen passenger cars were being produced in one year, and the demand for them steadily increased.

It was a little sad that so many well-known car names had disappeared – Mors, Delaunay-Belleville, Delage, Sheffield-Simplex, Napier, Itala, Richard Brasier, De Dietrich, to quote but a few, for these cars had seemed a part of our lives. But the past is the past and, always, new things take the place of the old.

Before the war, a factory controlled by William Lyons had produced a range of very interesting cars appealing mainly for their high performance. Now these cars, Jaguars, intruded among the big luxury cars with immediate success, their six-cylinder 3781 or 4235 c.c. shapely models, carrying a really comfortable, luxury body capable of very fast speeds – and their cost was relatively low compared with the prices of their rivals. It was something of a shock therefore, when this firm absorbed Daimlers, but that was nothing to the sensation when Jaguar joined up with B.M.C. in 1966.

All these big cars were at one end of a scale at the other end of which were the Minis, and all were genuine family cars, though for all different kinds of families. Between the two ends of the scale however there were a number of other cars from which to choose.

The British Ford factories now provided much better equipped Anglias and Prefects in 1953, improved these again in 1960, and then brought out the present Corsairs, Zephyrs, Zodiacs and Cortinas, whose clean lines immediately attract attention, in addition to their useful performance. In a way these were most 'unfordlike' Fords to those who consider all Fords as descendants of the Model T. But if you study the price it becomes apparent at once that Ford's policy remains unaltered, i.e. an exceptional value for money. For example the 1967 Zodiac which has a 3000 c.c. V6 engine, self-adjust-ing disc brakes, automatic gear change, costs £1,095 before tax, which compares well with other luxury cars.

Vauxhall's new Victor soon became popular after a lot of teething trouble, and is now available with automatic gears, and in 1966 this firm produced the Viscount with a six-cylinder, 3294 c.c. engine, automatic gears, electrically operated windows, and heated rear window, for £1,205 before tax.

Volkswagen increased the size of their 'Beetle' engine gradually until they had 1500 and 1600 c.c. models, both with four-cylinder, flat, air-cooled engines at the rear and more space for luggage. Subsequent models gradually departed from the familiar 'Beetle' lines and became more conventional, though the 'Beetle' is still the most popular.

Hillman, Rover, Humber, Austin, Morris, Triumph, Fiat, Citroën, Peugeot, Renault, Wolseley, could all provide cars of size and price in the intermediate range.

It is most interesting to note that most European cars now had engines of the same size as those little cars which appeared in such numbers just after the First World War. But the engines now had much more power. Way back in 1919 a 3000 c.c. engine was deemed small. Now it is good enough to power quite big five-seater cars, and is even thought to be large.

In direct contrast to European ideas the American manufacturers adhered to the big engine and big car, with at least five and sometimes six-seater cars which were wider, longer and fully automatic. That they adhered to the big engine was both logical and reasonable as long as taxation did not artificially increase the cost of fuel, or as long as the authorities did not tax cars according to their engine size. Larger engines never over-exerting themselves should always be more durable than small engines running near their limit, while a large engine provides more flexibility in top gear and

requires less change of gear ratios than a small one, and is therefore easier to drive. Fords, as one example, have engines of over 6000 c.c., one model having a length of 17 ft., a width of 6 ft. 5 ins. and height of 4 ft. 4 ins. The Cadillac Fleetwood with a 7030 c.c. V8 engine is nearly 19 ft. long.

With the increase of import duties after the war it became important for countries which were big enough to start producing their own cars. The Russians caused quite a sensation when they announced the Moskvitch, a four-cylinder 1360 c.c. car and the Volga, also with a four-cylinder engine but of 2445 c.c.

Aktiebolaget Volvo in Sweden produced a pleasant, medium sized car, the Volvo, with a 1778 c.c. four-cylinder engine as companion to Sweden's other car the S.A.A.B. – Svenska, Aeroplan, Aktiebolaget – an intriguing car for it had a three-cylinder, two-stroke engine of 841 c.c., a body of very modern shape, roomy accommodation for four people and a brisk performance.

Yet another unusual car came from Holland. Van Doorne's factory at Eindhoven commenced the manufacture of the DAF, short for Daffodil, a little car which seemed to be everything a novice could require, and it had a fully automatic gear. The two-cylinder, air-cooled 746 c.c. engine pulled well, was very easy to drive and could cruise nicely at 50 m.p.h. The automatic gear was unusual and consisted of a governor-controlled pulley sys-

tem with belts, and this naturally gave rise to considerable technical argument.

Japan's entry into the car industry provides ample food for thought. Originally the Japanese manufacturers assembled European cars. Then they became more adventurous, and today they have cars of their own manufacture and design. In 1933 the Nissan motor company was delivering Nissan trucks and the Datsun light car. Then it built a new plant to assemble the Austin A40 in 1953. In 1937 the Isuzu company was busy with trucks and buses, after which it assembled the Hillman Minx. Hino Diesel Industry, originated in 1917 to build heavy vehicles, turned to the assembly of the French Renault in 1952, while in 1954 the Fuji Precision Machinery firm took over manufacture of the Prince car.

As to Japanese originated cars, the Bellett is built by the Isuzu company on traditional lines with a four-cylinder engine of 1579 c.c. rated at 88 h.p. It has independent suspension front and rear, and disc brakes. The Isuzu company make a point of claiming that all accessories usually regarded as extras are included in the standard specification – vizors, safety belts, radio, fog lamps, etc. – while the tool kit is a real tool kit, not the ghostly vestige of the type usually provided today.

The Toyota firm make a 1500 c.c. and a 1800 c.c. Corona, a little 850 c.c. Publica with a flat twin 697 c.c. engine, a 1900 c.c. V8, and a 2600 c.c. engined

Below: The Bellett 1600 GT. Since the war Japanese car production has rocketed ahead, and now more than a dozen manufacturing concerns export cars and lorries to the Western World. By 1967 Japanese car production was greater than that of France and Britain combined.
Right top: The Oldsmobile Toronado, a six-passenger, two-door, racy saloon, has rapidly become very popular in the States.
Right bottom: The very popular and successful Triumph 2000. This model with the newer Triumph 1300 is fast carving a place for itself in the world's markets.

Crown. Daihatsu produce a four-cylinder 797 c.c. car and a similar 958 c.c., while Nissan now make the Sunny 988 c.c. and the 1299 c.c. Bluebird. The famous firm of Honda now export the attractive N-500 car, Hino produce a 1251 c.c. much resembling a Renault, and Prince Motors have the Mikados, a 2000 c.c. and a 2500 c.c. model. Mitsubishi, Subaru and Suzuki all build small cars on European lines. It is very apparent from this sudden burst of production that Japan is trying to enter the world market in a big way. In 1965 they produced 696,176 cars, and their production now exceeds British and French combined.

Czechoslovakia still build the Skoda and the Tatra, cars well known since 1920, the former, a rear-engined four-seater, about 60 h.p. priced at £540, tax included, and the Tatra, originally a rather big rear-engined car, now has a smaller version with 105 h.p.

To complete the list there is the three cylinder, two-stroke, front-drive Wartburg and the two-cylinder, air-cooled, front-drive Trabant from East Germany, the Austrian 660 c.c. air-cooled, twin-cylinder Steyr-Puch, and a Polish Syrena which resembles the Trabant but which has a larger 744 c.c. engine together with the Polish 2120 c.c. four-cylinder Warszawa.

This was all ample evidence that the world not only wanted cars, but that individual countries were thinking of their own designs at last. Furthermore, there are second-hand machines for those who cannot afford a new car, at prices well below their original cost, and there are also four-seater, three wheeled machines such as the Reliant, which may not rank technically as cars but are family transport at even less cost.

Development since the war has improved cars in every way, particularly in regard to the kind of detail which adds to comfort or convenience, but which is not immediately noticeable as a new arrangement of engine or transmission would be. Most cars now have windscreens which will not shatter into knife-like splinters if they receive a heavy blow. All cars have windscreen wipers, some with two-speeds, and also windscreen washers. Front seats can be adjusted, some for rake as well, while the back of the rear seat in an estate car can often be folded down flat to increase the load-carrying capacity of the car. Vizors are available to prevent dazzle from a low sun, as are also special lights to use in fog or when reversing.

When the first saloon bodies were fitted to the chassis they acted as amplifiers for every noise the engine made. This problem has been solved by a quite complicated system of sound damping which most people do not realize their car possesses. Body manufacture indeed has undergone vast change. Compare the bodies of paint and varnish days with those of today. The modern body today receives a thorough treatment of anti-rust phos-

Far left: Not only does the styling of the Rolls-Royce suggest tasteful luxury, but the car has an extraordinarily high performance. This Rolls-Royce Silver Cloud III can do over 100 m.p.h. without the passengers realizing it, and virtually noiselessly at that.

Left: The Ford Fairlane of 1966 is a fine example of modern American design, and makes an interesting contrast with the first Ford cars at the beginning of the century.

Bottom left: The lively Vauxhall Viva, provided to meet the European demand for a small, economical but fast car. The recognizable front has disappeared a long time ago.

Below: A 1966 Mercedes 230 SL. Combining lovely sleek, low lines, with the renowned Mercedes high performance this car is one of the most beautiful designs today.

Bottom right: More modern than modern—the controls and some of the mechanism of the Chrysler turbine-engined car.

Below: The firm of Jaguar, though a comparative new-comer to the motor industry, has made a great name for itself, largely because of the cars' performance and speed. This picture shows a Jaguar testing Dunlop tyres. It is cornering at full speed, and the roll is under full control.

Right: Motoring at its most exciting—the E-type Jaguar. Since the war Jaguars have adopted the philosophy of making elegance and performance doubly attractive by not charging the earth for their products. And it has paid them handsomely.

phate as a primer, the side, the underneath, and the mudguards a bituminous coating of anti-rust material, which also prevents the steel vibrating and deadens the noise. As many as four coats of a lacquer, may be applied, which will be really durable.

Ventilation and heating have become more scientific. In cold weather, warm air can be supplied to the screen and rear window, thus preventing icing-up and condensation. Controls are provided for the passengers or driver to adjust the temperature to suit themselves and, as the warm or cold air is supplied from a fan, the flow is not dependent on the speed of the car. Therefore the driver is less tired after a long run, his clear view from the driving seat to front or rear is maintained, and there are no draughts.

It may seem incredible but a modern body which is much more complicated than the body of 50 years ago is now constructed in one eighth of the time and costs one fourth its price.

Modern saloon bodies are remarkably strong and will become stronger still. But as yet no body will resist a crash at 70 m.p.h., even if this is the result of two cars travelling at 35 m.p.h. and colliding. Modern seats may not usually be leather upholstered, but the material used is far more durable than what we had in days of old, and needs very little maintenance. The fantastic amount of luggage a modern car can carry in the boot does not affect the handling of the car. The days are

gone in which one trunk on the rear carrier made the driver work hard to keep a steady speed.

Driving is so much easier and less tiring. All the larger cars can be provided with automatic gears, the driver having only to move a small lever on a quadrant in order to engage forward or reverse drive, or in order to delay the change to a higher gear. The clutch pedal is redundant therefore and only a brake and throttle pedal are necessary. The automatic gearbox was developed in America by General Motors and first used in 1939 for the Oldsmobile. Mercedes now have their own automatic gearbox which is becoming so popular that the firm estimates 100,000 will be fitted to their cars within the next two years. Even Minis have automatic gears, and even without automatic transmission gear-changing is easy, due to synchro-mesh, a mechanism first produced by General Motors for Cadillac.

Steering is often power-assisted for the big cars, and is finger-tip light compared with that on veteran or vintage cars and far more durable. Brakes are so durable and so reliable that people tend to neglect them scandalously. Gone are the old collection of rods and levers and balance gears, all have been replaced by a simple system of hydraulic control, while brake shoes can be made to adjust themselves. The mechanism can be power-assisted and there are devices to prevent a wheel locking at full braking pressure. Many cars have discs gripped by pincer-like shoes instead of the old drum and shoe affairs. Adjustment now is largely an affair for the service station, not the car owner.

Using the metal of the car as an earth-return system has simplified the ignition and lighting circuits, grouping the cables under strong sheaths has made for reliability. Carburetters are automatic, have air filters which reduce the noise caused by the air sucked into them. Ignition is controlled automatically. Water can no longer rush down the radiator vent pipe every time the driver brakes or accelerates because the filler cap is sealed with a spring-loaded valve. Everywhere in the world new and better metals are now used and bearings have become miraculously durable. All these details escape notice, are taken for granted even, but they are all important for the car's health.

Much thought is being given to ensure that cars are as safe as possible. Doors cannot fly open as easily in a crash as they did before. Bodies are sturdier, padding has been adopted wherever it can be fitted easily. The boss of the steering wheel has been reshaped to avoid injury to the driver's chest, the wheel rim can be flexible, or made to fracture under extreme shock. Much thought

Three examples of the Vauxhall's development.
Top: The Vauxhall Cresta of the mid 1950s.
Centre: The Victor of 1957.
Bottom: The 1967 VX/490. The modern Vauxhall is now a sleek and contemporary car, more in the manner of contemporary European design.

Right: But the pleasures of motoring may seem ephemeral. This is what going for a drive in a car increasingly means today. Nearly 20 million cars are produced annually, and our roads will soon not be able to contain them all. Maybe the pioneers were fortunate, driving their weird-looking cars along empty roads, with only the dust to hinder them.

has been given to the very difficult problem of how to avoid petrol fires when a car crashes. New tyre designs make skidding unlikely, new brake designs will not lock wheels yet give better control over the car. Safety belts will be standard equipment soon, and would have been before, had the right type been determined. Headlamps are less dazzling, and possibly something will soon be mounted in front of a car which will have a genuine buffer effect. In America a new form of toughened glass bends easily without breaking, which is a great improvement on the old form of toughened and laminated glass. Nevertheless safety still depends chiefly on the skill of the driver and always will.

Sixty years ago an output of 30 cars a week was considered good, in 1965 B.M.C. produced 886,077 vehicles, half of which were Minis, 1100s and 1800s; Fiat produced 1,013,588 vehicles; Volkswagen produced 747,060 vehicles; Citroën produced 485,496; Mercedes produced 17,400 cars; British Ford produced 505,168 cars; and Renault 563,000 vehicles. Rolls-Royce produced a stately 1,800 cars compared with the fantastic figures of American production – General Motors produced 4,949,388 cars, Ford a total of 2,565,737 cars, and Chrysler produced 1,467,553 cars.

So it goes on. Every year brings a new improvement as countless experimental departments work to make cars better. It may have taken seventy years to do, but it is a short time in which to perfect the modern car.

WHAT OF THE FUTURE?

One fact is certain, in the very near future, parking in cities will be almost impossible, and we are approaching that day very rapidly. Little cars have already been designed, which are electrically-powered, and which will take up less room when parking.

What will motoring be like at the beginning of the twenty-first century? It is difficult to prophecy with accuracy, or even to guess, but it seems certain that future development of the car will depend on two things – the supply of oil and the prosperity of the country. If petrol becomes scarce, which it must do someday, some other comparable fuel must be found. If money is still harder to earn and or costs are higher, manufacturers must concentrate on less expensive cars.

Nevertheless, whatever new problems have to be faced, it is probable that the engine we know today will still be in use, chiefly because it is well-known and well-understood, gives ample power for its weight, and is not expensive to manufacture. Taxation may restrict the size of engine used but we can guess that engines of absurdly small dimensions will produce enough power. The great success of the present-day 50 c.c. Japanese Honda engine for motor cycles proves that this could be so.

But if taxation does not limit the engine size or render the price of fuel unattainable for many, then the larger engine will come into its own (as it has already done in America), developing the same power at fewer revolutions, and lasting longer as a result.

But the normal reciprocating engine has strong rivals even today. Most important of these is the turbine which was first used for a car by Rovers of Solihull in 1950, and with which they have been experimenting carefully since then with very promising results. The great advantage of the turbine is its extreme simplicity. Briefly, air is sucked in by a fan into a cylinder, in which it is mixed with fuel and 'exploded'. The fierce rush of hot gas thus created is directed, by a nozzle, at a 'paddle wheel'. The paddle wheel is at one end of a shaft and at the other end are the gears which drive the wheels. No clutch, gearbox, carburetters, crankshaft, pistons or valves, the turbine consists of just the jet and paddle wheel. Of course there are refinements, fuel pumps, air, filters, heaters and the like, but the basic simplicity of the turbine remains.

A turbine-driven car is quieter and much smoother than any piston engine could ever be, because it develops steady power without any reciprocating parts; but its big drawback is that it consumes vast quantities of fuel and does not retard the car when the throttle is shut. This engine could very easily become the engine of the future, however, and that it shows great promise has already been realized. Fiat, Chrysler, General Motors and Renault all have experimental turbine cars.

Another type of engine which has definite potential

Top: The turbine engine shows great promise for the future, for it is light, small, simpler (having about one fifth the moving parts of the piston engine), needs no radiator or liquid cooling system. Also its electrical system is simpler, it is vibration free, and will run on almost any fuel.

Bottom: The controversial Wankel rotary engine.
1. Gas enters the inlet port, when the rotor is revolved.
2. The gas is compressed. 3. A spark at the plug ignites the compressed gas, and the explosion causes the rotor to revolve. 4. Exhaust gas escapes through the other port.

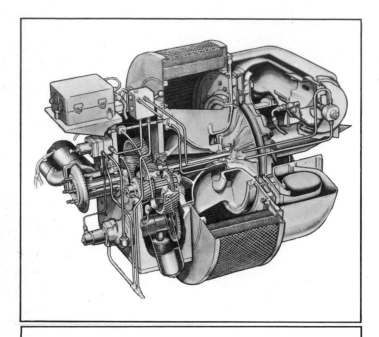

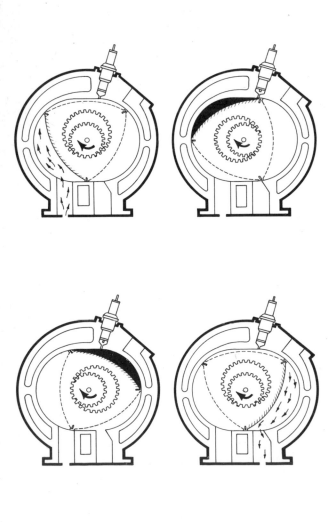

is the Wankel – it was conceived by Felix Wankel in 1954 and is now being further developed by the German N.S.U. firm – the older Neckarsulm. Moreover, the Japanese also are experimenting with this type of engine.

This engine has a triangular rotor in a special shaped casing. Taking one side of the rotor at a time, the first part of its movement sucks in fuel which, as the rotor continues to revolve, is compressed and fired by a normal plug, thus driving the rotor round. For the remainder of the circle used gas is allowed to escape as the rotor opens a port in the chamber. As this cycle takes place, for each face of the rotor there are three impulses per revolution, therefore an almost continuous drive. The rotor shaft drives the usual gears and through them the wheels. More experiment is necessary before this engine gives its best results, part of the difficulty being the seals between rotor and chamber, equivalent to the piston rings, and control of the engine lubricating oil to prevent a very smoky exhaust. But the promise is there.

Of course if petrol becomes very scarce some form of steam engine may have to be further developed, for the defects of steam propulsion for cars are not insurmountable. Electricity may also have its chance, depending on battery development. As it is some very useful little 'runabouts' with electric motors are being tested for short journeys in and around cities, handy little cars which could well be in great demand if big cars are eventually banned from city centres.

And stretching imagination to the limit, it is quite possible power may be transmitted to a car from a distant power station, thus making most of the mechanism we know today, and fuel stations even, unnecessary. In fact it is possible that power may eventually be transmitted to cars without wires. For instance, in 1965, a small helicopter was kept aloft for 10 hours solely on power transmitted to it in a microwave beam from the ground. Wireless power transmission is nearing the stage at which it may find practical application.

Even now some ambitious proposals for transport in cities are being considered. By 1980 we may be accustomed to the idea of living in cities in which people will move around in automatic, driverless taxis, driven by inserting a metallic token into the taxi, which will set it off on its journey running along lines and choosing the right spot to branch off; electronically guided buses; high-speed monorails; and moving pavements. Inter-city travel might consist of a motor-way network for average speeds of 60 m.p.h., or a 400 m.p.h. airliner network with rapid city-centre connections from airports, and 'air-cushion' trains on the Hovercraft prin-

Top: One version of the Chrysler turbine-engined car. Swept back aerodynamic styling gives a distinctive appearance to the rear of the car. Tail lights, indicator and reversing lights are recessed in large chromium mountings which are structurally reinforced and act as the car's bumper.

Bottom: Two tiny electric cars, designed to save space and provide transport in busy, crowded cities. In the foreground is a Trident, opened to show the simplicity of the mechanism, and in the background is a Scamp. Both can do up to 35 m.p.h. They operate on two 12-volt batteries with a carbon pile regulator.

Top left: These three cars for the future were shown by General Motors at the New York World's Fair. Top is the Runabout, a three-wheeled utility vehicle for the future city-dweller, featuring a built-in shopping cart system. Centre is the Firebird IV for fast, comfortable cross-country cruising on automatic highways. Bottom is the GM-X, a two-passenger, high-performance coupe appealing to the enthusiast.
Bottom left: The Pininfarina Sigma safety car. This prototype features many interesting measures, including sliding doors, an efficient ventilating system, retractable steering-wheel and much soft padding.

ciple, with speeds of 250 m.p.h. or more. It would seem that already legs are becoming redundant.

But whatever system wins the battle the car for family motoring will presumably change radically. Streamlined in shape, it will have all-round vision and will probably be built of plastic or fibreglass or some material even stronger, stronger than steel maybe, yet sufficiently flexible to cushion severe blows without damage to itself. Windows and screens will be made of a similar flexible material though transparent, and will be able to yield and yet return to form much as rubber would do.

Control will be almost entirely automatic, pushbutton in fact, except that the steering and the brakes will be more directly under the driver's control, but taking less effort to use than now. Steering may even be by tiller with servo-assistance, and there will be no need to open windows in hot weather or close them when it is cold, since air conditioning will be extremely efficient inside the car.

It is possible to foresee a device based on radar which would automatically prevent collisions or even one car coming within twelve inches of another, and a variation

of that same device which would warn the driver that another car is approaching though not yet in sight, and that he must consequently reduce speed. As a result of much experiment General Motors of America produced in 1966 the 'Driver's Aid'. When this is fitted to a car the driver can receive warning messages about the conditions of roads or traffic ahead while he is driving along, and in turn can radio ahead to a service station, summon help, or even ask for advice. It may well be a simple matter to order accommodation or a meal at an hotel miles ahead and receive acknowledgement.

Messages from low frequency transmitters attached to traffic signs at the side of the road will be received on a panel inside the car. Cables or magnets could be buried in the road, so that a driver could be signalled to turn right or left at the correct moment, and thus keep to a pre-selected route without trouble or worry.

In another experiment by the General Motors research department a car was driven entirely by a computer several miles along a highway. A card punched with the car's route and destination is inserted in a slot in a 'black box' inside the car, and thereafter all directions about the route are given and transmitted to the car automatically.

It seems unlikely that maximum speed will increase, because that would entail more skill than the average person is capable of maintaining, but average speeds will mount all the same because the roads themselves will be so much improved. There will be no cross road junctions, no short radius blind turns, while road surfaces will be such as to make skidding a thing of the past. And, the cause of many accidents, pedestrians will be segregated from vehicles on all busy roads. All features of main roads will be standardized, in all countries signals and facilities will be similar, so that one will be able to drive from, say, Edinburgh to Rome, and scarcely realize the roads had changed.

Motoring in the future has exciting and intriguing prospects, but one thing can be prophesied with absolute certainty. Driving a motor car will give our grandchildren as much, maybe even greater, pleasure than we have today. Moreover, they will look back on the cars of the 1960s with just as much amusement and interest as we extend to the cars of the pioneer days.

ACKNOWLEDGEMENTS

Austin Motor Company Limited.
Author's Collection.
Autocar.
British Hovercraft Corporation Limited.
British Motor Corporation Limited.
David Brown.
Bullock & Turner Limited.
Burberrys Limited.
Camera Press Limited.
Carrozzeria Pininfarina.
Central Press Photos Limited.
Chrysler International S.A.
Citroën.
C. Conolly-Smith.
Daimler-Benz A.G.
Dunlop Rubber Co. Limited.
Eldon Studios.
Fiat.
Ford (Great Britain).
Ford (U.S.A.)
Fox Photos Limited.
General Motors Limited.
Guy Griffiths.
V. K. Guy.
Paul Hamlyn Library.
Indianapolis Motor Speedway Corporation.
Jaguar Cars Limited.
Louis Klemantaski.
George H. Lanchester.
Mercedes-Benz.
Montagu Motor Museum.
Motor.
D. Napier & Son Limited.
The Nuffield Organization.
Peugeot.
Picturepoint Limited.
Press Association Limited.
Renault Limited.
Peter Roberts.
Rolls-Royce Limited.
Rootes Motors Limited.
Rover Company Limited.
The Science Museum.
Smithsonian Institution.
Vic Stacey.
Standard Triumph International Limited.
Syndication International.
United Press International (U.K.) Limited.
Vauxhall Motors Limited.
Veteran Motor Car Club of America.
Volkswagen Motors Limited.

INDEX